Themen 2

Lehrwerk für
Deutsch als Fremdsprache

Glossar
Deutsch-Englisch

bearbeitet von Sandy Mason und Alan G. Jones

Max Hueber Verlag

6. 5. 4. | Die letzten Ziffern bezeichnen
1994 93 92 91 90 | Zahl und Jahr des Druckes.
Alle Drucke dieser Auflage können, da unverändert, nebeneinander
benutzt werden.
1. Auflage
© 1986 Max Hueber Verlag, D-8045 Ismaning
Umschlagillustration: Dieter Bonhorst, München
Gesamtherstellung: Pustet, Regensburg
Printed in the Federal Republic of Germany
ISBN 3–19–041372–X

Introduction

This Glossary follows the pattern adopted in the Glossary for Themen 1. For each chapter, the page-by-page vocabulary is followed by contrastive notes designed specially to help you, the English-speaking learner. At the end of this book you will find an index showing all the items dealt with in the Contrastive Notes for either volume.

Not included in this Glossary is the vocabulary for the short story "Die Gefährlichkeit der Rasensprenger" and for the texts in the Arbeitsbuch. This omission is deliberate. The "Rasensprenger" story is intended for straight reading, without reference to glossary or dictionary; in this way you can get used to reading over unfamiliar words and guessing their meaning from the broader context, from the root of the word or from an illustration. The same is true for some of the additional texts in the Arbeitsbuch. However, you will find that among those texts there are some which are quite demanding, providing the more ambitious student with a challenge and an opportunity to start using a "real" dictionary.

Lektion 1

Seite 8	Page 8
die Person, -en	person
blond	blonde
klein	short, small
lustig	jolly
sympathisch	likeable, congenial
	→ see contrastive notes
schlank	slim
dünn	thin
schwarzhaarig	black-haired
jung	young
nett	nice
traurig	sad
ruhig	calm
attraktiv	attractive
intelligent	intelligent
dumm	dumb, stupid
unsympathisch	disagreeable, uncongenial
glauben	to believe
cm = der Zentimeter	centimeter
der Clown, -s	clown
der Pfarrer, -	vicar, parson, pastor
das Fotomodell, -e	model
die Psychologin, -nen	(woman) psychologist
der Psychologe, -n	psychologist
die Hexe, -n	witch

Seite 9	Page 9
also	→
Also, ich meine ...	Well, I think ...
die Lösung, -en	solution
das Photo, -s (also: Foto)	photograph
das Ehepaar, -e	married couple
passen	to fit
viel	much
das Gedächtnis	memory
das Bild, -er	picture

4

genau	→
Sehen Sie die drei Bilder genau an.	Look closely at the three pictures.
nächste	next
weiterlesen	to read on

Seite 10 | Page 10

der Teil, -e	part
gehören zu	to belong to
runde ← rund	round → see contrastive notes
blauen ← blau	blue
oval	oval
braun	brown
schmal	narrow
schwarz	black
lang	long
das Familienbild, -er	family picture
haben von	→
Die große Nase hat er vom Vater.	He has his father's big nose.
die Mutter, ⸚	mother
rot	red
grün	green
gelb	yellow
weiß	white
grau	grey

Seite 11 | Page 11

meistens	mostly, most often
Eine schöne Frau ist meistens dumm.	Most beautiful women are stupid.
bescheiden	modest, unassuming
schwer	with difficulty
Ein kleiner Mann findet schwer eine Frau,	A short man has difficulty finding a wife.
gesund	healthy
gemütlich	→ see contrastive notes
sparsam	thrifty
die Ehefrau, -en	wife
treu	true, faithful
küssen	to kiss
die Sorge, -n	worry
der Feind, -e	enemy

voll	full
still	silent, calm
Stille Wasser sind tief.	Still waters run deep.
tief	deep
reich	rich
Reiche Männer sind meistens häßlich.	Most rich men are ugly.
richtig	right
wahr	true
der Unsinn	nonsense
freundlich	friendly
interessant	interesting
das Mädchen, -	girl

Seite 12 — Page 12

der Tip, -s	tip
der Stil, -e	style
die/der Bankangestellte, -n	bank employee
tragen	to wear
dezent	modest, subdued
die Kleidung	clothing
bis	until
der Mut	courage
frisch	up-to-date
sportlich	sporty
die Mode, -n	fashion
so	→
So ist Karin zu uns gekommen.	Karin came to us looking like this.
das Haar, -e	hair
die Brille, -n	glasses
das Make-up	make-up
die Bluse, -n	blouse
der Rock, ⁻e	skirt
die Frisur, -en	hairstyle
nicht mehr, kein/keine mehr	no longer, not any more
Sie trägt keine Brille mehr.	She doesn't wear glasses any more.
weich	soft
die Kontaktlinse, -n	contact lense
die Größe, -n	size
ideal	ideal
der Pullover, -	pullover, sweater
dazu	with this

6

der Strumpf, ⸚e	stocking
die Kniestrümpfe	knee socks
die Typberatung, -en	style analysis
die Redaktion, -en	editorial staff
der Schuh, -e	shoe
vorher	previously
die Jacke, -n	jacket
schicken	to send
hellblau	light blue
dunkelblau	dark blue

Seite 13   Page 13

der Anzug, ⸚e	suit
die Krawatte, -n	tie
das Hemd, -en	shirt
das Kleid, -er	dress
was für ein?	what kind of? what sort of?
	→ see contrastive notes
der Sportschuh, -e	tennis shoe, casual
das Kleidungsstück, -e	article of clothing
anziehen	to put on (clothes)

Seite 14   Page 14

das Telegramm, -e	telegram
die Deutsche Bundespost	Federal Postal Service
das Druckhaus, ⸚er	printing house, printer
konnte (← können)	could
telefonisch	by telephone
erreichen	to reach
ankommen	to arrive
Hbf. = der Hauptbahnhof, ⸚e	main train station
abholen	to pick up
die Papierfabrik, -en	paper factory
gerade	just
kennenlernen	to meet
persönlich	personally
ja	→ see contrastive notes
endlich	finally
Dann lerne ich Sie ja endlich persönlich kennen.	Well, then I'll finally get to meet you in person.

sich freuen	to be pleased
wie	how
erkennen	to recognize
der Mantel, ⸚	coat
dunkel	dark
klar	clear
der Haupteingang, ⸚e	main entrance
die Karte, -n	card
übermorgen	the day after tomorrow
mal	→ see contrastive notes
der Ausgang, ⸚e	exit
der Bahnsteig, -e	platform → see contrastive notes
die Ordnung, -en	order
In Ordnung.	Sounds good.
Einverstanden.	Agreed.

Seite 15 / Page 15

richtig	correct
von	of
der Ehemann, ⸚er	husband
unterstreichen	to underline
das Adjektiv, -e	adjective
unsportlich	unathletic
elegant	elegant
das Psycho-Spiel	psychological game
tolerant	tolerant, open-minded
der Arbeitskollege, -n	co-worker, colleague
der Punkt, -e	point
jede/jeder/jedes	every → see contrastive notes
denken	to think
manche/mancher/manches	some
erziehen	to bring up, to raise
alle	all
so	→
Alle Kinder essen so.	All children eat that way.
die U-Bahn = Untergrundbahn	subway, underground
eben	→
Manche Leute sind eben verrückt.	Some people are just crazy.

Seite 16	Page 16
sicher	surely, certainly
ehrlich	honest
genau	exact, precise
pünktlich	punctual
stark	strong
das Vorurteil, -e	prejudice
kritisieren	to criticize
angenehm	agreeable
wirklich	really
egal	→
Viele Probleme sind Ihnen egal.	About many problems you don't care at all.
offen	open
der Typ	type
der Babysitter, -	babysitter
lieb	loving
die Bezahlung	pay
der Job, -s	job
mal	times
2 bis 3 mal pro Woche.	2 to 3 times a week.
die Chance	chance

Seite 17	Page 17
arbeitslos	unemployed
möglich	possible
der/die Arbeitslose, -n	unemployed person
	→ see contrastive notes
das Geld	money
der Irokese	iroquois
der Punk, -s	punk, punker
die Irokesenfrisur	iroquois hairstyle
das Arbeitslosengeld	unemployment benefit
der Beamte, -n	official
das Aussehen	(physical) appearance
jeden Morgen	every morning
das Badezimmer, -	bathroom
tragen	to wear
die Mitte	middle
mittlere	middle (adjective)

stehen	to stand
dafür	for this reason
die Meinung, -en	opinion
das Stellenangebot, -e	job offer
normal	normal
sich	yourself (with the polite form "Sie")
wiederkommen	to come again
sabotieren	to sabotage
die Stellensuche	job search
der Arbeitgeber	employer
zufrieden	satisfied
das Leben	life
schwer	difficult
... haben Heinz das Leben schwer gemacht.	... made Heinz' life difficult.
ärgern	annoy
kündigen	to give notice; to dismiss
	→ see contrastive notes
die Stelle, -n	position, job
meist	most
die Buchhandlung, -en	bookshop, bookstore
der Prozeß, Prozesse	lawsuit
führen	→
einen Prozeß gegen jemanden führen	to bring a lawsuit against someone
der Rechtsanwalt, ⁻e	lawyer

Seite 18	Page 18
der Arbeitnehmer, -	employee
z. B. = zum Beispiel	for example
also	→
Er ist also arbeitslos.	So he is unemployed.
sonst	otherwise, or else
der Leser, -	reader
frühere/früherer/früheres	former
gar nicht	→
Heinz will gar nicht arbeiten.	Heinz really doesn't want to work at all.
wie	like
die Reihenfolge	order, sequence
stehen	to be (located, found, written)
In welcher Reihenfolge stehen diese Informationen im Text?	In what order are these facts in the text?

die Universität, -en	university
die Moschee	mosque
eigentlich	actually
die Jeans	jeans
die Punkhexe, -n	punk witch

die Entscheidung, -en	decision
die Leistung, -en	performance
selbst	self
der Fehler, -	mistake
sicher	sure, certain
zahlen	to pay
ganz	quite, completely, totally
lügen	to lie
meinetwegen	as far as I'm concerned
gleich	→
Das ist mir gleich.	It's all the same to me.
die Sache, -n	→
Das ist seine Sache.	That's his business.
verlangen	to demand

Contrastive notes

sympathisch (page 8): *Ich finde sie sympathisch.* means *I like her.* The phrase can be turned around, too, making the object of sympathy into the grammatical subject: *Sie ist mir sympathisch.* Unlike *gefallen*, which can build similar phrases, *sympathisch sein* is not normally used to describe feelings towards ideas or propositions, but only towards people. Its opposite is *unsympathisch.*

runde (pages 10 and 131): Unlike English, adjectives in German take an ending when they come in front of their noun. As you will gather from the table on page 131 in the Kursbuch, the ending depends on several things: the gender of the noun, its case, whether it is singular or plural and whether its article is definite or indefinite.
Don't try to learn the table on page 131 of the Kursbuch by heart; use it rather to look up endings you are not sure about. The actual learning is in this case best done "synthetically": by memorizing whole sentences of the type found in the Kursbuch on page 11.
Note that there is no ending at all when an adjective comes as a *Qualitativergänzung*, i. e. separated from its noun (→ Themen 1, Kursbuch page 129).

11

gemütlich (page 11): Applied to a person, *gemütlich* has the meaning of *pleasant, good-natured.* More generally, it is used to indicate *cosy, comfortable* or *informal. Hier ist es gemütlich.* means *There is a nice atmosphere here.*

was für (page 13): This means *what sort of* or *what kind of.* To ask the question *what for?* (i. e. *for what purpose?*), German uses *wofür?.*

ja (page 14): Like *doch, ja* can be used as a modifier indicating that the statement is not being made for its factual information but in order to convey something about the relationship between the two speakers: willingness to keep it friendly, a hope that it may become more personal and less formal, etc. Without this modifier, the statement *Dann lerne ich Sie endlich persönlich kennen.* would, in this context, be all but impossible. If made, it would probably be perceived as a rather disconcerting hint at some forgotten incident or remark, perhaps as a mysterious threat.

mal (page 14): *mal* is short for *einmal*, which literally means *once.* In the phrase *Dann sehe ich Sie ja endlich mal.*, however, *mal* is used in its most frequent function: as a modifier to tone down the importance of the event.

der Bahnsteig (page 14): In Themen 1 we learned that *Platform five* is *Gleis fünf.* Now we have another word for *platform.* In fact, *Gleis* is really *track*, whereas *the platform* itself is *der Bahnsteig.* So the phrase *Gleis fünf* literally means *track five*, but this is how German indicates where a train is. If you think about it, the English *The train now standing on platform five* ... is – one hopes – inaccurate!

jede/jeder/jedes (pages 15 and 130): This word covers the meaning of both *every* and *each.* Together with *diese/dieser/dieses* and *manche/mancher/manches*, it belongs to a group of *Artikelwörter* ("article words", words with the function of articles) which take the same endings as the definite article *der, die, das.*

der Arbeitslose (page 17): A number of adjectives can be turned into nouns while holding on to their adjective endings. One of these is *der Arbeitslose*, which should be thought of as *der arbeitslose Mann.* Accordingly, in *Akkusativ* it is *den Arbeitslosen*, in *Dativ dem Arbeitslosen*, while with the indefinite article *(ein)*, the new adjective-noun takes the forms *ein Arbeitsloser/einen Arbeitslosen/einem Arbeitslosen.* When reference is made to unemployed women, the appropriate forms are *eine Arbeitslose (Nominativ* and *Akkusativ)* and *einer Arbeitslosen (Dativ)*, and with definite articles *die Arbeitslose* and *der Arbeitslosen* respectively.

kündigen (page 17): This means the ending of a work contract, no matter by which side. *Er hat gekündigt* means *He gave in his notice*, but *Man hat ihm gekündigt* would indicate *He was dismissed.*

Lektion 2

der Zoodirektor, -en	zoo director
der Löwe, -n	lion
die Angst, ¨e	fear
das Fernsehen	television (the medium, not the TV set)
der Bundeskanzler, -	Federal Chancellor
der/die Sportler/in	athlete
gewinnen	to win
die Goldmedaille, -n	gold medal
verdienen	to earn
der Nachtwächter, -	night watchman
nachts	nights, at night
der Hund, -e	dog
der/die Dolmetscher/in	interpreter
die Sprache, -n	language
das Ausland	foreign countries

weil	because → see contrastive notes
die Chefhexe	head witch
wollte (← wollen)	wanted
der Wunschberuf, -e	dream career, desired career
die Jugend	youth
von	out of
je	→
von je 1000	out of every 1000
der Schulabgänger, -	school leaver
nennen	to name
nannte (← nennen)	named
der Elektriker, -	electrician
der Kfz-Mechaniker	motor vehicle mechanic
das Kfz (= Kraftfahrzeug)	motor vehicle
der/die Büroangestellte, -n	office worker
die Bankfachkraft, -kräfte	bank clerk
die Freizeit	free time, leisure time
der Funk- und Fernsehtechniker	radio and TV technician
der Installateur, -e	electrician, plumber

der Maschinenschlosser	fitter
der Maurer	bricklayer
der Maler	painter
der Tischler	carpenter
die Sprechstundenhilfe, -n	doctor's assistant
die Friseuse	hairdresser
die Kindergärtnerin	Kindergarten/nursery school teacher
die Masseuse, -n	masseuse
die Krankengymnastin, -nen	physiotherapist
die Sozialpädagogin, -nen	educational social worker
die Hauswirtschafterin, -nen	home economist
die Technische Zeichnerin, -nen	tracer
als	as
der Nebensatz, ⸚e	dependent clause
das Präsens	present tense
das Präteritum	simple past tense

Seite 24 / Page 24

die Umfrage, -n	opinion poll, survey
das Sprachinstitut, -e	language school
mußte (← müssen)	had to
das Dolmetscherdiplom, -e	interpreter's diploma
noch nie	never yet
selbständig	independently
am liebsten	→
Mein Chef möchte am liebsten alles selbst machen.	My boss prefers to do everything himself.
die Autowerkstatt, ⸚en	garage
mußte (← müssen)	had to
der Automechaniker, -	motor mechanic
dazu	for that
der Bruder, ⸚	brother
es besser haben	to have it better
durfte (← dürfen)	was permitted
bestimmen	to decide
der Bürokaufmann (-kaufleute)	clerk
schmutzig	dirty
sauber	clean
nach Hause	→
Er geht nach Hause.	He goes home.
der Möbelpacker, -	furniture remover

14

der Unfall, ⁻e	accident
schwer	heavy
tragen	to carry
praktisch	practically
das Familienleben	family life
sollte (← sollen)	was supposed to
der Großvater, ⁻	grandfather
die Ausbildung	training course
die Kinderkrankenschwester, -n	children's nurse
obwohl	although
die Überstunden (plural)	overtime
die Zukunft	future
unzufrieden	dissatisfied

Seite 25   Page 25

das Modalverb	modal verb, "helping" verb
gleich	right away
anderes	→
nichts anderes	nothing else
noch	→
noch eine Lehrerin	(yet) another teacher
die Arbeitszeit, -en	work hours, schedule
die Schule, -n	school
schwer	→
schwer arbeiten	to work hard
der Traumberuf, -e	dream career

Seite 26   Page 26

	for this whole page
	→ see contrastive notes
das Zeugnis, -se (Abschlußzeugnis)	report
das Abschlußzeugnis, -se	school leaving report
der Unterricht	teaching
die Klasse, -n	class
die Realschule, -n	secondary school with emphasis on science and modern languages
der Realschulzweig, -e	Realschule stream (of a comprehensive school)
erhalten	to receive
folgend	following

der Pflichtunterricht	obligatory class
die Religion, -en	religion
Englisch	English
die Gesellschaftslehre, -n	community studies
die Erdkunde	geography
die Sozialkunde	social studies
die Mathematik	mathematics
die Physik	physics
die Biologie	biology
der Sport	sports, gym
die Kunst, ¨e	art
die Bemerkung, -en	remark
das Versäumnis, -se	absence
entschuldigt	excused
unentschuldigt	unexcused
der Klassenlehrer, -	form teacher
der Schulleiter, -	head teacher, principal
die Erläuterung, -en	explanation
befriedigend	satisfactory
ausreichend	adequate (passing)
mangelhaft	poor
ungenügend	unsatisfactory
die Hochschule, -n	university, college
das Abitur	leaving certificate (end of Gymnasium)
der Abiturient, -en	student who has completed the abitur
die Fachhochschule, -n	polytechnic
die Fachschule, -n	technical college
das Fachgymnasium, -gymnasien	technical school
die Fachoberschule, -n	secondary technical school
die Berufsschule, -n	college of further education
die Lehre, -n	apprenticeship
das Gymnasium, Gymnasien	selective senior secondary school
das Schuljahr, -e	School year
der Realschulabschluß, -abschlüsse	Realschule leaving certificate
die Hauptschule, -n	general secondary school (for pupils not going to Realschule or Gymnasium)
der Hauptschulabschluß, -abschlüsse	Hauptschule leaving certificate
die Grundschule, -n	primary school, grade school

korrigieren	to correct
die Aussage, -n	statement
das Schulsystem, -e	school system
wenn	if, when → see contrastive notes
wählen	to choose
die Zeugnisnote, -n	grade
die Note, -n	grade
das Schulfach, -̈er	school subject
aussuchen	to pick out, select
der Realschüler, -	Realschule student
zu Ende	at an end, finished
verschieden	various
die Möglichkeit, -en	possibility
die Gesamtschule, -n	comprehensive school
aufhören	to end, to make an end
überlegen	to consider
mindestens	at least
das Prozent, -e	percent
nach	after
das Studium	course of studies

die Lehrstelle, -n	apprenticeship
die Schulzeit	schooldays
der Mann, -̈er	husband
sei (← sein)	be (imperative) →
Sei doch nicht so dumm!	Don't be silly!
der Akademiker, -	university graduate
das Rollenspiel, -e	role play
die Schwester, -n	sister
als	than
früher	→
eine bessere Ausbildung als früher	better training than before
das T-Shirt	T-shirt
saubermachen	to clean
manchmal	sometimes
fertig	finished
tun	to do

17

was	→
Ich weiß nicht, was ich tun soll.	I don't know what to do.
nirgends	nowhere
die Bewerbung, -en	application
die Antwort, -en	answer, reply
negativ	negative
verlangen	to require
es heißt	it says
der Antwortbrief, -e	letter of reply
außerdem	what is more
wegnehmen	to take away
niemand	no one
der/die Jugendliche, -n	young person
offiziell	officially
die Statistik, -en	statistics
der Zweck	point
Das hat doch keinen Zweck.	There is no point in it.
da	→
Da geht man drei Jahre zur Schule ...	You go to school for (another) three years ...
trotzdem	in spite of that
das Examen, -	examination
der Büroberuf	office job
die Erzieherin, -nen	nursery teacher
so	→
so Andrea	according to Andrea
wechseln	to change
sich bewerben (ich bewerbe mich)	to apply
es klappt	it works, it goes right

Seite 29	**Page 29**
weiter	→
... geht sie vielleicht weiter zur Schule.	... she may stay on at school.
uninteressant	of no interest
die Worte (plural)	→
mit Ihren Worten	in your own words
der Polizist, -en	police officer
sicher	secure
zufällig	by chance
letzte/letzter/letzte	last
Spaß machen	to be fun, enjoyable

das Diplom, -e	diploma
die Reise, -n	trip

die Rechnungsabteilung, -en	accounting division
die Elektronikindustrie	electronics industry
zusammenarbeiten	to work together
das Unternehmen	enterprise
das Gehalt, ⁼er	salary
das Urlaubsgeld	holiday pay
die Sportmöglichkeit, -en	sports facilities
ausgezeichnet	excellent
die Karrierechance, -n	opportunity for career advancement
versprechen	to promise
der Arbeitsplatz, ⁼e	position, workplace
die 5-Tage-Woche	5 day week
ca. = circa	approximately
dynamisch	dynamic
die Persönlichkeit, -en	personality
perfekt	perfect
das Team, -s	team
lösen	to solve
vorwärts	→
vorwärts kommen	to get on, to get ahead
unter	→
unter der Nummer	at this number
schicken	to send
immer	→
immer größer	bigger and bigger
der Geschäftskontakt, -e	business contact
die Chefsekretärin, -nen	director's secretary, P. A.
die Sprachkenntnisse (plural)	language ability
weitere/weiterer/weiteres	other, additional
die Fremdsprache, -n	foreign language
vorbereiten	→
Sie bereiten Termine vor.	You schedule appointments.
der Termin, -e	appointment
der Kunde, -n	customer
das Inland	home country
die Messe, -n	trade fair
der Vertrag, ⁼e	contract

das Wort, -e	→
mit einem Wort: ...	in a word: ...
die Arbeitsatmosphäre	work atmosphere
bieten	to offer
das Monatsgehalt, ⁻er	monthly salary
die Betriebsrente, -n	firm's pension
die Kantine, -n	canteen
das Möbelunternehmen, -	furniture company
das Geschäft, -e	store
ganz	whole → see contrastive notes
der Verkaufsdirektor, -en	sales director
dringend	urgently
mehrere	several
die Berufserfahrung, -en	work experience
das Betriebsklima	working conditions, atmosphere at work
die Sozialleistungen (plural)	fringe benefits
KG = Kommanditgesellschaft	limited partnership
das Postfach, ⁻er	post office box
sollen	→
Sie soll gut Englisch sprechen.	A good command of English is required.

Seite 31 — Page 31

die Firma, Firmen	company
die Personalabteilung, -en	personnel division
Betr. = betrifft	concerning, re:
geehrte	→ see contrastive notes
die Dame, -n	lady
hiermit	herewith
seit 1976	since 1976
die Aufgabe, -n	task
der Lebenslauf, ⁻e	curriculum vitae
geb. = geborene	born, née
der Vorname, -n	first name, given name
geboren	born
1962–1966 („1962 bis 1966")	from 1962 to 1966
das Dolmetscherinstitut, -e	interpreter's institute
das Sprachpraktikum, -praktika	language placement
Fa. = Firma	company
der Import, -e	import
der Export, -e	export
die Heirat	marriage

20

der Exportkaufmann (-kaufleute)	export businessman
die Abendschule, -n	night school
der Sekretärinnenkurs	secretary's course
die Abschlußprüfung, -en	final examination
die Prüfung, -en	examination
die Industrie- und Handelskammer	chamber of Industry and Commerce
geprüft	qualified
die Scheidung, -en	divorce
jetzige/jetziger/jetziges	current
noch einmal	once more
vom ... bis zum ...	from the (date) to the (date)
der April	April
der Juni	June
der Personalchef, -s	personnel director
zurückkommen	to return

Seite 32 — Page 32

notieren	to make a note of
die Notiz, -en	note
brutto	gross (pay)
verwenden	to use
samstags	Saturdays
die Fahrt, -en	drive
die Haltestelle, -n	bus stop, tram stop
der Bus, -se	bus
allein	alone
kaum	hardly, few
der Kontakt, -e	contact
das Geschäft, -e	business
das Huhn, ¨er	hen (here used as an insult)
die Wunschliste, -n	request list
die Berufswahl	career choice
der Verdienst	earnings
sozial	social
die Sicherheit	security
leicht	light
die Karriere, -n	here: career prospects
das Prestige	prestige
der Arbeitsort, -e	place (city, town) of work

21

Sag mal, ...	Tell me, ...
das Angebot, -e	offer
nochmal	further
ganz	→
Ein Angebot gefällt mir ganz gut.	I rather like one offer.
besonders	special
annehmen	to accept
mal	→ see contrastive notes
etwas	something

Contrastive notes

weil (pages 23 and 132/133): Whenever a clause starts with *weil (because),* this clause will be a *Nebensatz,* the personal form of its verb taking the second verb position (at the end of the clause; see section 2, pages 132/133). The same applies to clauses introduced by *wenn* and *obwohl. weil, wenn* and *obwohl* are called *Subjunktoren.*

However, not all words which introduce new clauses in a sentence are *Subjunktoren:* some are *Konjunktoren,* and the clause they introduce is a *Hauptsatz* and has the same word order as you would expect in English. Frequently used *Konjunktoren* include *aber, und,* and *denn.* Note that all these words can take on other functions as well, besides serving as *Konjunktoren.*

Schools and colleges (page 26): The chart shows the various types of school and college in Germany. There are very few comprehensive schools *(Gesamtschulen)*; most pupils go to one of the three types of secondary school shown here.

For the *Hauptschulabschluß,* no formal examination is required.

wenn (page 27): This *Subjunktor* can mean either *when* or *if,* depending on the context, though the dual meaning generally presents more problems to Germans speaking English than the other way around. English-speakers need to distinguish it clearly from *wann,* which is the question *When?.* Examples:
Wenn es regnet, bleibe ich zu Hause.
Wann fahren Sie nach Bonn?

ganz (page 30): Used as an adjective, *ganz* means *whole.* But as an adverb modifying another adjective, it means *quite.* Examples:
in der ganzen Bundesrepublik – in the whole of West Germany
ganz wichtig – quite important.

As an adverb modifying a verb, *ganz* means *totally*. You will find an exercise on the various uses of *ganz* later on in Lektion 4 (*Arbeitsbuch,* Lektion 4, exercise 23).

Sehr geehrte Damen und Herren (page 31): Note that formal letters always start with *Sehr geehrte(r)* rather than *Liebe(r)*, which can only be used when writing to someone you know.

mal (page 33): This is another example of *mal* being used to soften a sentence, to make it sound more casual. *Na ja, mal sehen* could be rendered by English *Well, we'll see.*

Lektion 3

Seite 36

Page 36

der Februar	February
das Programm, -e	channel
die ARD = Arbeitsgemeinschaft der öffentlichen Rundfunkanstalten der Bundesrepublik Deutschland	umbrella organization of West German radio and TV
die Tagesschau	News
die Expedition, -en	expedition
das Tierreich	animal kingdom
die Großstadt, ̈e	big city
der Tod	death
die Reportage, -n	report
das Motorradfahren	motorcycle riding
schwer	heavy
die Maschine, -n	here: motorcycle
sicher	safely
Sport-Extra	sports special
der Weltcup	World Cup
der Ski-Weltcup	World Skiing Championship
der Riesenslalom	giant slalom
die Ferien (plural)	vacation
die Sendung, -en	show, broadcast
die Kindersendung, -en	children's programme
der Zeichentrickfilm, -e	cartoon film

der Wohnwagen, -	caravan, trailer
das Regionalprogramm, -e	regional programme
das Werbefernsehen	TV commercials, advertising
Hessen, Berlin, Bayern etc.	radio and TV stations which together form the ARD
der Rundfunk	radio and TV
heiter	humorous
das Beruferaten	career guessing
das Sonderdezernat	special department
die Rache	revenge
der Krimi, -s	detective story
die Regie	direction
heroinsüchtig	addicted to heroin
das Heroin	heroin
ermorden	to murder
der/die Tote, -n	dead person
der Kommissar, -e	police superintendent
die Spur, -en	clue
die Tagesthemen	themes for the day, Newsnight
die Kultur	culture
der Moderator, -en	host, presenter
der Soziologe	sociologist
der Gewerkschafter, -	trade/labor union member
der Zoo, -s	zoo
die Filmkamera, -s	film camera
wildlebend	living in the wild
aufnehmen	to take a film, a photograph etc.
die Kanalisation, -en	sewer system
sich gewöhnen an	to become accustomed to, to get used to
die Reihe	serial
die Haut, ⁻e	skin
spannend	exciting
real	real
der Hintergrund, ⁻e	background
der Handel	trade
das Rauschgift, -e	narcotic drug
die Droge, -n	drug
die Drogenszene	drug scene
der Sozialhelfer, -	social worker
zugute kommen	to prove beneficial for
Das kommt dem Film zugute.	That benefits the film.
übertreiben	exaggerate

realistisch	realistic
der Herointote, -n	heroin victim
die Mitternacht	midnight
vergangen	→
im vergangenen Jahr	in the past year
die Mission	mission
glaubwürdig	believable, credible
die Melodie, -n	melody
die Welt	world
die Weltreise, -n	trip around the world
klangvoll	tuneful
der Calypso	calypso
führen	to lead
die Gruppe, -n	group
der Atlantik	Atlantic Ocean
das Gesundheitsmagazin, -e	health magazine
die Praxis	surgery, (doctor's) practice
fremdartig	strange
die Nähe	vicinity
in der Nähe	around, near
normalerweise	normally
der Fall	case
... was normalerweise der Fall ist.	... which is normally the case.
doppelt	doubly
der Beitrag, ⁻e	here: part, item
der Elternteil, -e	one of the parents
die Kosten (plural)	cost, expense
die Organisation, -en	organization
der Leiter, -	director, head
städtisch	municipal (funded by the town council)
das Lehrerproblem, -e	teacher's problem
das Schülerproblem, -e	student's problem
das Thema, Themen	theme
der Lieblingsschüler, -	favorite student, teacher's pet
die Teleillustrierte	TV magazine
die Unterhaltung, -en	entertainment
der Gast, ⁻e	guest
die Diätküche	diet cuisine
der Tip, -s	tip
hungern	to starve
der TV-Koch	TV cook
das Pfund, -e	pound

leicht	light
das Rezept, -e	recipe
davon	→
eines davon	one of these
chinesisch	Chinese
die Nudel, -n	noodle
braten	to grill
das Gewürz, -e	seasoning
bekannt	well-known
der Star, -s	star
singen	to sing
der Hit, -s	hit
das Auslandsjournal	foreign journal
der Bericht, -e	report
die Analyse, -n	analysis
die Herzchirurgie	heart surgery
der/die Herzkranke, -n	person with a heart condition
aktuell	topical
die Sprechstunde, -n	consultation time, surgery
das Journal	journal
der Trend, -s	trend
der Mini	mini skirt
die Hose, -n	trousers, pants
der Hosenanzug, ̈e	pants-suit, trouser suit
die Modefarbe, -n	fashionable colour
untreu	unfaithful
der Spielfilm, -e	feature film
der Liebhaber	lover

Seite 37 — Page 37

die Uhrzeit, -en	time
das Fernsehprogramm, -e	TV programme guide
die Politik	politics
ähnlich	similar

Seite 38 — Page 38

der Leserbrief, -e	letter from a reader
der Fernsehabend, -e	evening of TV
der Mist	here: rubbish
der Techniker, -	technician

das Diskussionsthema, -themen	topic for discussion
sich ärgern über	to become irritated, annoyed
	→ see contrastive notes
sich freuen auf	to look forward to
fehlen	to be missing
der Pfeffer	pepper; here: spice, pizzazz
herzlich	heartfelt, warmest
der Glückwunsch, ¨e	congratulation
Herzlichen Glückwunsch!	Congratulations!
die Sendezeit, -en	broadcast time
sich interessieren für	to be interested in
wofür, worauf, worüber	→ see contrastive notes
der Kriminalfilm, -e	detective film
die Angabe, -n	data
der Kinofilm, -e	feature film
die Komödie, -n	comedy
das Volksstück, -e	dialect play
die Showsendung, -en	light entertainment show
die Quizsendung, -en	game show
der Western, -	western
regional	local, regional
der Ratgeber, -	advice programme
der Problemfilm, -e	film dealing with a certain issue
die Musik	music
die Wissenschaft, -en	science
die Technik	technology
die Literatur	literature
die Wirtschaft	economy
die Jugendsendung, -en	youth show

Seite 39	Page 39
anmachen	to turn on
mal	→ see contrastive notes to Lektion 2
kommen	→
Was kommt denn jetzt?	What's coming on now?
die Nachrichten (plural)	news
dasselbe	the same
können	→
Kann sein.	Maybe so.
nun mal	→ see contrastive notes
die Unterhaltungssendung, -en	entertainment show

wenigstens	at least
..., ja?	..., okay?
jedesmal	always, every time
gleich	the same
mögen	→
Mag sein.	Maybe so.
ein bißchen	a little bit
regelmäßig	regularly
vor allem	above all
von	→
Von mir aus.	I don't mind.

Seite 40   Page 40

die Karikatur, -en	cartoon
die Natur	nature
früher	earlier, before
kaputtmachen	to destroy
die Spielsachen (plural)	playthings, toys
soviel	so much
die Limonade, -n	soda pop, lemonade
ungesund	unhealthy
der Sohn, ¨e	son
die Mama	mama, mummy
Peng!	Bang!
aggressiv	aggressive

Seite 41   Page 41

der Hunger	hunger
der Durst	thirst
ob	whether
überhaupt	at all
überhaupt nicht	not at all
gewiß	certain, sure
der Hut, ¨e	hat
die Ecke, -n	corner
hätt' = hätte	would have → see contrastive notes
wär' = wäre	would be → see contrastive notes
stehlen	to steal
schlagen	to hit, to beat
der Brei	pulp

der Bursche, -n	lad
durstig	thirsty
die Freud' = Freude, -n	joy
das Lied, -er	song
solche/solcher/solches	such → see contrastive notes
die Tür, -en	door
die Seite, -n	page

Seite 42   Page 42

ach	oh
mit jemandem gehen	to go steady with someone
würdest	→ see contrastive notes
nie mehr	never again
der Text, -e	here: song lyrics
laufen	to run
verlieren	to lose
verlieben	to fall in love
üben	to practise
das Wörterverzeichnis, -se	word list
der Liedtext, -e	song lyrics
schicken	to send
der Verlag, -e	publishing house
das Lektorat, -e	editors' department
der Autor, -en	author
mitsingen	to sing along
das Trinklied, -er	drinking song
die Popmusik	popular music
der Gedanke, -n	thought
erraten	to guess
vorbeifliegen	to fly past
nächtlich	of the night
der Schatten, -	shadow
der Jäger, -	hunter
erschießen	to shoot
dabei	→
Es bleibt dabei, …	It's settled, …

Seite 43   Page 43

der Straßenkünstler, -	street artist
der Musikant, -en	musician

der Maler, -	painter
der Schauspieler, -	actor
die Schauspielerin, -nen	actress
ziehen	to move
von	→
von Stadt zu Stadt	from city to city
malen	to paint
der Asphalt	pavement, sidewalk
einige	some, several
20jährig	20 year-old
die Straßenpantomimin, -nen	street mime artist
der Alltagstrott	everyday routine
feucht	damp
der Rathausmarkt	square in front of the town hall in Hamburg
warten	to wait
der Zuschauer, -	spectator, audience
auspacken	to unpack
die Sache, -n	thing
beginnen	to begin
die Vorstellung, -en	performance
imaginär	imaginary
der Umschlag, ⁼e	envelope
tun	here: to throw
der Papierkorb, ⁼e	waste basket
da sein	to exist
weinen	to cry
das Pantomimenspiel, -e	mime show
der Bart, ⁼e	beard
sich aufregen	to get excited, worked up
so etwas	that sort of thing
müßte	ought to, should
verbieten	to forbid
sammeln	to collect
der Pfennig, -e	pfennig (100 to 1 Mark)
spielen	here: to perform
die Asphaltkunst	pavement art, sidewalk art
gewöhnlich	normally, usually
die Asphaltkarriere, -n	pavement career
der Krach	row
der Schnellkurs, -e	rapid course

vor	→
vor sechs Monaten	six months ago
der Platz, ⁻e	place
die Fußgängerzone, -n	pedestrian zone
die Ladenpassage, -n	shopping arcade
das Einkaufszentrum, -zentren	shopping centre
der Einkauf, ⁻e	shopping
stehenbleiben	to stop
sich ausruhen	to relax, to rest
das Straßentheater, -	street theatre
verboten	forbidden
die Geschäftsleute (plural)	business people
sich beschweren	to complain
der Zigeuner, -	gypsy
der Nichtstuer, -	layabout, bum
unruhig	restless
der Boden	ground
den Boden unter den Füßen verlieren	to lose one's footing

Seite 44	**Page 44**
der Pantomimenkurs, -e	mime course
der Streit	quarrel
der/die Mitbürger/in	fellow citizen
das Musizieren	music-making
musizieren	to make music
das Ordnungsamt, ⁻er	public order office
die Lizenzregelung, -en	license regulation
der/die Bürger/in	citizen
fragen	to ask
sich anmelden	to register
die Lizenz, -en	license, permit
beantragen	to apply for
einmal	once
die Kulturwüste, -n	cultural desert
angeblich	supposedly
die Kulturstadt, ⁻e	cultural city
allmählich	gradually
die Kunstfreiheit	artistic freedom
das Konsumzentrum, -zentren	consumer's center
einfach	simply
sich setzen	to sit

31

sich unterhalten	to converse, to chat
das Kommunikationszentrum, -zentren	communication center
etwas tun gegen	to take action against
unterschreiben	to sign
offen	open
ein offener Brief	an open letter
der Stadtrat	city council
V. i. S. d. P. = Verantwortlich im Sinne des Pressegesetzes	published by; lit.: responsible under the terms of the Press Act

Seite 45	Page 45
der Straßenzigeuner, -	"street gypsy"
der Konzertsaal, -säle	concert hall
das Kaufhaus, ̈-er	department store
eigentlich	actually
fehlen	to be lacking
Mir würde ... etwas fehlen.	I would miss something.
die Stadtmitte	city centre, downtown
der Geschäftsmann, -leute	businessman
stören	to disturb
der Geschäftsverkehr	store traffic
der Ort, -e	place
nötig	necessary
dagegen sein	to be against
die Qualität	quality
leise	soft
der Supermarkt, ̈-e	supermarket

Contrastive notes

sich ärgern über (pages 38 and 134): Some verbs require an object pronoun referring back to their subject in order to complete their meaning. *Ich ärgere* is incomplete, you must say *ich ärgere mich* (literally: *I annoy myself*). Note that for the third person *(er, sie)* and the polite *Sie*, the reflexive pronoun required is always *sich*.

Some of these so-called reflexive verbs can be completed with other than reflexive pronouns, too. Example: *Günter Weiher ärgert sich über den Moderator. – Günter Weiher schickt dem Moderator seinen Leserbrief und ärgert ihn damit.*

Other reflexive verbs can only be used with a reflexive pronoun. Example: *Elfi Ammer freut sich auf die nächste Sendung.*

32

wofür, worauf, worüber (pages 38 and 134): We saw in Lektion 1 that *was für* means *what sort of* and that for *what for?*, German uses *wofür?*. Here are some more similar question words. Note that the preposition *(für, auf, über)* is often determined by the verb and does not necessarily appear to „make sense". After *sich interessieren*, the preposition is always *für*; *sich freuen auf* means *to look forward to*, and *sich freuen über* means *to be happy about*; after *sich ärgern*, the preposition required is *über*.
Besides the question words *wofür, worüber* etc., there is a group of pronominal words: *dafür, darüber* etc. Example: *Interessierst du dich für Krimis? – Nein, dafür interessiere ich mich nicht.*

nun mal (page 39): This phrase means something like *You'll have to accept that*... It appeals to the communication partner to be sensible and not to close his eyes to reality.

solche (page 41): This is the plural form of *so ein, so eine*. For *solche Lieder*, we should probably say in English *songs like these*.

wäre, hätte (pages 41 and 135): This is a short way of saying *would be, would have* – or, in the context of the songs on this page, *if it had ... it would be*.
These verbs are in a tense known in German as *Konjunktiv II*, which is used to indicate a hypothetical situation. We use it very little in English, but it does exist in phrases such as *if I were rich*. You can find the full tense on page 135.

würdest (page 42): For most verbs, German uses *würde* plus the infinitive to form the *Konjunktiv II* (e. g. *ich würde kommen*). Only for a small number of short verbs, the verb itself changes. These are the verbs shown on page 135 in the table headed *Formen*.

Lektion 4

Seite 48	Page 48
der Test, -s	test
wie	→
so gut wie	as good as
der Preis, -e	price
inkl. = inklusive	including
MWSt. = die Mehrwertsteuer, -n	value added tax
die Steuer, -n	tax

die Motorleistung, -en	engine performance
KW = das Kilowatt, -	kilowatt
PS = die Pferdestärke, -n	horsepower
die Höchstgeschwindigkeit	maximum speed
km = der Kilometer, -	kilometer
km/h = Kilometer pro Stunde	kilometers per hour
der Verbrauch	(gasoline/petrol) consumption
l = der Liter, -	liter, litre
l/100 km = Liter auf 100 km	litre per 100 km
das Gewicht	weight
der Kofferraum, ⁻e	trunk, boot
die Versicherung, -en	insurance
das Superbenzin	premium gasoline/petrol
das Normalbenzin	regular gasoline/petrol
der Durchschnitt, -e	average
im Durchschnitt	on average
die Reparatur, -en	repair
niedrig	low
hoch	high
stark	strong
preiswert	reasonably priced
am höchsten	→ see contrastive notes
die Geschwindigkeit, -en	speed
der Benzinverbrauch	gasoline/petrol consumption
schwächer	→ see contrastive notes
der Motor, -en	engine
als	→
Er hat einen schwächeren Motor als der Micra.	Its engine is less powerful than the one in the Micra.
dafür	here: on the other hand
genauso ... wie	just as ... as

Seite 49	**Page 49**
der Ärger	trouble
die Bremse, -n	brake
das Öl	oil
der Spiegel, -	mirror
der Reifen, -	tyre/tire
das Bremslicht, -er	brake light
das Fahrlicht, -er	headlight
kaputt	broken, out of action

weiterfahren	to drive on
abschleppen	to tow away
der Tank, -s	(gas/petrol) tank
leer	empty
die Panne, -n	breakdown
der Unfallwagen, -	emergency vehicle
die Tankstelle, -n	gasoline/petrol station
der Scheibenwischer, -	windscreen/windshield wiper

Seite 50 / Page 50

der Wagen, -	car, automobile
ziehen	to pull
Die Bremsen ziehen nach links.	The foot brake pulls to the left.
links; linke/linker/linkes	left
sonst	else
Sonst noch etwas?	Anything else?
hinten	back
der Nachmittag, -e	afternoon
heute nachmittag	this afternoon
wahrscheinlich	probably
schwierig	difficult
fertig	ready, finished
sich erinnern	to remember
los	→
Was ist denn los?	What's the matter? What's wrong?
laufen	to run
die Handbremse	handbrake
vorne, vorn	front
rechts	on the right
aufmachen	to open
Noch was? Noch etwas?	Anything else?
tanken	to put in gasoline/petrol
waschen	to wash
früh	→ see contrastive notes
heute früh	this morning
mittag	noon, midday

Seite 51 / Page 51

die Rechnung, -en	bill
der Arbeitslohn, ⁻e	labor charge

der Bremsbelag, ⁻e	brake lining
das Stück, -e	piece → see contrastive notes
zwei Stück	two
einstellen	adjust
das Material, -ien	material, parts
das Handbremsseil, -e	handbrake cable
die Summe, -n	sum
der Betrag, ⁻e	amount
reparieren	to repair
extra	extra, additional
weiterschreiben	here: to extend (the dialogue) in writing
spielen	here: to act out
folgende/folgender/folgendes	following
interessieren	to interest
überzeugen	to convince
unwichtig	unimportant
Verzeihung.	I'm sorry.
der Tankwart, -e	gasoline/petrol station attendant
vollmachen	to fill

Seite 52   Page 52

das Blech, -e	sheet metal
die Autoproduktion	automobile production
früh	early
werden	→ see contrastive notes
das Montageteil, -e	part to be assembled
der Lastwagen, -	truck, lorry
die Karosserie, -n	automobile body
automatisch	automatically
daraus	out of this
pressen	to press
das Dach, ⁻er	roof
der Boden, ⁻	floor
das Seitenteil, -e	side panel
usw. = und so weiter	etc.
das Blechteil, -e	sheet metal part
zusammenschweißen	to weld together
von	by → see contrastive notes
der Roboter, -	robot
lackieren	to paint

das Mal, -e	→
mehrere Male	several times
spritzen	to spray
gegen	against
der Rost	rust
schützen	to protect
fertig	to completion
montieren	to assemble
fertig montiert	assembled to completion
das Rad, ¨er	wheel
der Sitz, -e	seat
prüfen	to test
von ... aus	starting from
eigene/eigener/eigenes	own
der Käufer, -	buyer
zusammensetzen	to put together
das Karosserieblech, -e	sheet metal for the automobile body
zuletzt	lastly

Seite 53   Page 53

die Karosserieabteilung, -en	automobile body division
die Maschine, -n	machine
die Montageabteilung, -en	assembly division
der Schluß, Schlüsse	end
zum Schluß	finally
das Autohaus, ¨er	car dealer's
gerade	right now
der Besen, -	broom

Seite 54   Page 54

der Beschäftigte, -n	employee
die Fahrschule, -n	driving school
die Behörde, -n	authority
der Straßenbau	road construction
die Garage, -n	garage
der Kfz-Handel	motor vehicle trade
die Dienstleistung, -en	service
die Zulieferindustrie, -n	supply industry
über	→
über 4 Millionen	more than 4 million

die Autofabrik, -en	automobile factory
die Autoteilefabrik, -en	automobile parts factory
das Amt, ⁻er	public office
das Autogeschäft, -e	car dealer's
der Ort, -e	place
das Elektroteil, -e	electrical part
die Prüfabteilung, -en	testing division
monoton	monotonous
das Werkzeug, -e	tool → see contrastive notes
der Autoreifen, -	tyre/tire
die Materialprüfung, -en	material testing
der Versand	dispatch
die Schweißerei, -en	welding division
der Knopf, ⁻e	button
drücken	to push
kleben	to stick
der Stundenlohn, ⁻e	hourly wages

Seite 55   Page 55

das Haushaltsgeld	housekeeping money
monatlich	monthly
das Nettoeinkommen, -	net income
der Arbeitnehmerhaushalt, -e	employee household
das Einkommen, -	income
insgesamt	in all
der Verkehr	transport
der Hausrat	household goods
die Bildung	education
die Heizung, -en	heating
der Strom	electricity
das Gas	gas
u. a. = und anderes	etc.
die Körperflege	personal hygiene
die Esparnis, -se	saving
der Lohn, ⁻e	wages
das Gehalt, ⁻er	salary
die Abrechnung, -en	statement
der Zeitraum, ⁻e	period
Über-Std. = die Überstunde, -n	overtime
der Zuschlag, ⁻e	bonus
der Bruttoverdienst	gross earnings

38

der Abzug, ⁻e	deduction
die Lohnsteuer, -n	income tax
die Kirchensteuer, -n	church tax → see contrastive notes
kath. = katholisch	catholic
die Krankenversicherung, -en	health insurance
die Arbeitslosenversicherung, -en	unemployment insurance
die Rentenversicherung, -en	pension insurance
gesamt	total
der Netto-Verdienst	net earnings
steuerfrei	tax free
das Fahrgeld	travelling expenses
auszahlen	to pay out
der Betrag, ⁻e	total amount
auszuzahlender Betrag	payable amount, net pay
errechnet	calculated
das Datum	date
das Zeichen, -	here: initials
ausgeben	to spend
IG = die Industriegewerkschaft, -en	industrial union → see contrastive notes
die Keramik	ceramics
chemisch	chemical
etwa	approximately
die Verhandlung, -en	negotiation
der Druck	printing
das Tarifgespräch, -e	pay talk → see contrastive notes
rund	around, approximately
die Druckindustrie, -n	printing industry
der Metallarbeiter, -	metal worker
das Metall, -e	metal
der Streik, -s	strike
streiken	to strike
damit	here: thus (this brings the total to)

Seite 56 / Page 56

die Hauptsache, -n	main thing
die Kasse, -n	cash
die Kasse stimmt	here: the pay is right
die Fließbandarbeit	assembly-line work
gelernt	skilled
der Metzger, -	butcher
der Fließbandarbeiter, -	assembly-line worker

ausbilden	to train
CO_2 = das Kohlendioxyd, -e	carbon dioxide
der Schweißer, -	welder
das Hochband, ̈er	high conveyor belt
die Halle, -n	here: factory workshop
heißen	here: to mean
vorbeilaufen	to move past
die Sekunde, -n	second
der Wechselschichtarbeiter, -	movable swing-shift worker
machen	→
Sein Stundenlohn macht 16,06 DM.	His hourly wage rate is 16,06 DM.
der Monatslohn, ̈e	monthly wages
die Essenspause, -n	meal break
bezahlen	to pay
dreimal	three times
der Tarif, -e	wage agreement
nach Tarif	according to the wage agreement
frei bekommen	→
Er bekommt zehn Tage frei.	He gets ten days off.
der Arbeitstag, -e	workday
plus	plus
das Taschengeld	pocket money
dazubekommen	to earn extra
das Weihnachtsgeld	Christmas bonus
das Krisenjahr, -e	crisis year
halten bei	to keep with
das Vergnügen, -	pleasure
froh	glad, happy
das Monatsende, -n	end of the month
das Bankkonto, -konten	bank account
mitarbeiten	here: to work also
der Winterurlaub	winter vacation
der Sommerurlaub	summer vacation
wie	→
wie jeder Arbeiter	like every worker
die Fabrikwohnung, -en	company apartment
günstig	favourably priced
vermieten	to let, to rent out
die Nebenkosten (plural)	additional expenses
die Rationalisierung, -en	rationalization
entlassen	to let go
der Vorarbeiter, -	foreman

raus = heraus	out
die Produktion	here: production side
die Monotonie	monotony
als	→
als Betriebsrat	as a works council member
der Betriebsrat, ⁼e	works council member
	→ see contrastive notes
die Seite, -n	side

Seite 57   Page 57

die Überschrift, -en	heading
der Tarifvertrag, ⁼e	wages agreement
die Verbindung, -en	connection

Contrastive notes

am höchsten (pages 48 and 136): To indicate *biggest, fastest* etc., German, like English, adds
-*st*; but it doesn't stop there.
If the superlative is free-standing, it is used with the preposition *am* and the ending -*en*
added to the -*st*-: *Der Peugeot ist am längsten.*
But if it precedes the noun, the adjective ending must be used:
Er hat die höchste Geschwindigkeit.

schwächer (pages 48 and 136): To form comparative adjectives, German, like English, adds
-*er*. But unlike English, German can add -*er* to any adjective, no matter how long it is. If the
adjective precedes its noun, the usual adjective ending must be added to the -*er*. Examples:
Dieser Motor ist schwächer.
Das Auto hat einen schwächeren Motor.
Note the use of *wie (as)* and *als (than)* in comparisons:
Er fährt so schnell wie der Peugeot.
Er fährt schneller als der Polo.

früh (page 50): *Morgen* can mean *morning* and *tomorrow* – so how do you say *tomorrow
morning* in German? The answer is *morgen früh.*

Stück (page 51): Literally this means *piece* or *item*, but it is used also where English would
not translate it. *Geben Sie mir fünf Stück.* means *Give me five (of them).*

werden (pages 52 and 137): Where English uses the verb *to be* to form the passive *(The wheels
are protected.)*, German uses the verb *werden (Die Räder werden geschützt.)*. From the chart

41

on page 137 you can see that the original object of an active sentence becomes the subject of the passive statement.

Also on page 137, note some other uses of *werden*.

von (page 52): In the passive, the original subject of the statement is often dropped altogether, or it becomes, by means of the preposition *von*, a *freie Angabe*.

das Werkzeug (page 54): This can either be used to denote a single tool or a set of tools needed for a particular job.

Kirchensteuer (page 55): Germans who are members of one of the major churches pay a church tax which is collected alongside income tax.

IG = die Industriegewerkschaft (page 55): Germany has sixteen large unions, each covering a whole industry rather than a single craft. This means that normally an employer will have to deal only with one union.

das Tarifgespräch (page 55): German firms normally hava a wages agreement with the appropriate union, which is legally binding and covers terms of employment, holiday entitlements etc.

der Betriebsrat (page 56): All medium and large firms in Germany have a works council which is a forum for resolving disputes. The word *Betriebsrat* is used both for the council itself, and for an individual member of it.

Lektion 5

Seite 60	Page 60
versuchen	to try
abnehmen	to lose weight
die Pünktlichkeit	punctuality
aktiv	active
anders	different
zuviel	too much
schon wieder	→ see contrastive notes
zu	→
zu spät kommen	to come (too) late
lachen	to laugh

Seite 61

gern mögen
leiden können
   Unhöfliche Leute kann ich nicht leiden.
unhöflich
reden
der Humor
aggressiv
natürlich
zu ärgern
entschuldigen

Page 61

to like → see contrastive notes
to be able to put up with
   I can't stand impolite people.
impolite
to talk
sense of humor
aggressive
natural
→ see contrastive notes
to excuse

Seite 62

das Telefon, -e
der Eheberater, -
kritisieren
der Kindergarten, ¨
sich duschen
ausmachen
wecken
hängen

Page 62

telephone
marriage counselor
to criticize
Kindergarten
to shower
to turn off
to wake (someone) up
to hang

Seite 63

das Paar, -e
genießen
sollen
die Untersuchung, -en
daß
der Kühlschrank, ¨e
der Anfang, ¨e
die Anschaffung, -en
die Waschmaschine, -n
während
das Ehejahr, -e
das Interview, -s
das Baby, -s
hoffen
bald
aufhören

Page 63

couple
to enjoy
should
investigation
that → see contrastive notes
refrigerator
beginning
acquisition
washing machine
during
year of marriage
interview
baby
to hope
soon
to stop

Seite 64

Page 64

sich verloben	to become engaged
daß	→ see contrastive notes
der/die Verlobte, -n	engaged person, fiancé(e)
die Liebe	love
die Ehe	marriage
dagegen sein	to be against
töten	to kill
überzeugt	convinced
glücklich	happy
tot	dead
dafür sein	to be in favour

Seite 65

Page 65

der Garten, ⸚	garden
grillen	to grill, barbecue
die Sauce, -n	sauce
spielen	to play
kontrollieren	to check
die Hausaufgabe, -n	homework
schimpfen	to complain
die Unordnung	disorder
die Ruhe	rest
entweder ... oder ...	either ... or ...
sich wohl fühlen	to feel well
kaputt	here: exhausted

Seite 66

Page 66

der Familienabend, -e	family evening
die Großeltern	grandparents
der Besuch	visitor → see contrastive notes
zusammen sein	to be together
der Ton, ⸚e	tone of voice
Der Ton macht die Musik!	It's all in the way you say it!
müde	tired
ja	→
Du kannst ja im Bett noch lesen.	You can read in bed a while, so it won't be that bad.
Gute Nacht.	Good night!

schon
  Ich gehe ja schon.

→
I'm going already!

Seite 67 | Page 67

langsam — slowly

wie

  Du fährst wie ein Verrückter.

→
You're driving like a madman.

halten

  Halt den Mund!

→
Shut up!

der Minidialog, -e — mini-dialogue

auswählen — to pick out, to choose

dauernd — constantly → see contrastive notes

die Telefonrechnung — telephone bill

Seite 68/69 | Page 68/69

die Generation, -en — generation

das Sofa, -s — sofa

das Foto, -s — photograph

von links — from the left

die Großmutter, ÷ — grandmother

die Urgroßmutter, ÷ — great-grandmother

die Ururgroßmutter, ÷ — great-great-grandmother

die Ururenkelin, -nen — great-great-grandchild (f.)

liegen

  Zwischen ... liegen 88 Jahre.

→
88 years lie between ...

die Erziehung — education, upbringing

das Altersheim, -e — home for the aged

die Jugendzeit — youth

hart — difficult, hard

richtig

  richtige Eltern

→
proper parents

vergaß ← vergessen — forgot

dachte ← denken — thought

starb ← sterben — died

damals — at that time

schließlich — finally

  Mit 30 hatte sie schließlich sechs
  Kinder.

  In the end, she had six children by the
  time she was 30.

das Kindermädchen, - — nursemaid

erzogen ← erziehen — raised

gutbürgerlich	solidly middle-class
das Elternhaus	home
wirtschaftlich	financial
kannte ← kennen	knew
der Privatlehrer, -	private tutor
sich unterhalten	to converse
etwas	somewhat
fremd	distant, remote
wenn	→ see contrastive notes
schlief ← schlafen	slept
gab ← geben	→
es gab	there was, there were
die Ohrfeige, -n	slap in the face
als	→ see contrastive notes
bis	until
die Kinderschwester, -n	children's nurse
fand ← finden	here: considered
die Kindheit	childhood
das Gesetz, -e	law
das Kriegsjahr, -e	war year
sich fühlen	to feel
Sie fühlte sich sicher.	She felt secure.
der Wunsch, ⸚e	wish
der Rebell, -en	rebel
zog aus ← ausziehen	moved out
bekam ← bekommen	→ see contrastive notes
Mit 17 Jahren bekam sie ein Kind.	At 17 she had a child.
früh	soon
blieb ← bleiben	stayed
halfen ← helfen	helped
die/der Verwandte, -n	relative
deutlich	clearly
unterhielten ← sich unterhalten	conversed
die/der Erwachsene	adult
unmöglich	impossible, unthinkable

Seite 70 — Page 70

verschieden	different
kritisch	critical
der Partner, -	partner
der Enkel, -	grandson

der Tischlermeister, -	master carpenter
gest. = gestorben	died
der Handwerker, -	craftsman
Westfalen	Westphalia
fast	almost, nearly
fast allein	almost single-handedly
die Volksschule	basic primary and secondary school
höchstens	at most
die Mietwohnung	rented apartment
der Kundenkontakt, -e	customer contact
das Präteritum	→ see contrastive notes

Seite 71	Page 71
der Urgroßvater, ⁼	great-grandfather
das Fragespiel, -e	question game
der Onkel, -	uncle
die Tante, -n	aunt
der Cousin	cousin
die Cousine	cousin
der Neffe, -n	nephew
die Nichte, -n	niece
die Enkelin, -nen	granddaughter
der Schwager, ⁼	brother-in-law
die Schwägerin, -nen	sister-in-law
der Genitiv	→ see contrastive notes
aufpassen auf	to look after

Contrastive notes

schon wieder (page 60): Literally, *schon* means *already*; in combination with *wieder* it denotes a repetition that comes too soon, sooner than expected. (You may notice that when some Germans speak English, they will insert the word *already* into a sentence where it does not belong. This is because the word *schon* is used far more frequently in German than its equivalent in English.)

gern mögen (page 61): This means *to like*, and needs to be distinguished from *ich möchte*. (*Ich mag Rheinwein.* is a general statement, but *Ich möchte Rheinwein.* is an indication of what you would like right now.)

zu ärgern (pages 61 and 138): A number of German verbs can have as an *Ergänzung* a so-called *Infinitivsatz mit zu*. This is not a *Nebensatz*, because there is neither a subject nor the personal form of a verb in it; only the infinitive of a verb, preceded by *zu*.

The English equivalents of most of these verbs can be followed by a similar construction with *to*. Note, however, that German does not require a *zu* after the modal verbs *wollen, mögen, müssen* and *dürfen*, while their English counterparts require an infinitive with *to (to want to, to like to, to have to, to be allowed to do sth.)*.

daß (pages 64 and 138): This is equivalent to the <u>unstressed</u> English *that* as in the phrase *I think that he will come.* In German, *daß*-clauses always have the personal form of the verb at the end: *Stimmt es, daß Burglind geheiratet hat?* In other words, *daß* is a *Subjunktor* like *weil, wenn* and *obwohl.*

(Do not confuse *daß* with *das,* which, among other things, is the German word for the <u>stressed</u> *that* in phrases like *That was a long way.*)

der Besuch (page 66): This can cause problems because it can either refer to the abstract *the visit* or to the person *the visitor*.

dauernd (page 67): The verb *dauern* means *to last,* and *dauernd* as an adverb has the sense of *constantly, repeatedly.*

als (pages 68/69 and 140): *Als* is used to mean *when* referring to past events. However, it is replaced by *wenn* when repeated actions in the past (or in the timeless present) are described, e.g. customs, habits etc. Examples:

Als sie 15 Jahre alt war, kam sie in eine Mädchenschule.

Wenn zum Beispiel die Mutter nachmittags schlief, durften die Kinder nicht laut sein und spielen.

This use of *als* is of course quite different from its use after a comparative to mean *(faster, bigger ...) than.*

bekommen (page 68): To English speakers this is a false friend: it means *to receive/get,* <u>not</u> *to become* (which in German is *werden*).

Präteritum (pages 70 and 139): As you will see from the tables on page 139, there are two types of simple past tense, *stark* and *schwach*. It is simplest to learn by heart those which are *starke Verben* and work on the basis that any others are *schwache Verben.* You will find a list of *starke Verben* on page 152 of the Kursbuch which covers all verbs that occur in Themen 1 and Themen 2.

The simple past tense is generally used in writing rather than in speech; you will find it particularly in newspaper reports and in scientific articles (or, of course, History books!). In speech, German tends to use the Perfect Tense, which you already know, apart from a small number of short verbs where the simple past is so familiar that it is used more frequently.

Genitiv (pages 71 and 140): For nouns with an *Artikelwort*, the genitive form is as shown in the clip-note. From the table on page 140, you will see that after a Genitive *Artikelwort*, the adjective ending is *-en*. For proper nouns (names), German indicates posession by simply adding an *-s* (*Gabis Zimmer, Rolfs Auto* etc.). Frequently, spoken German avoids using the Genitive, and uses *von* instead.

Lektion 6

Seite 74 — Page 74

die Landschaft, -en	landscape
das Klima	climate
heiß	hot
kühl	cool
der Regen	rain
es regnet	it's raining → see contrastive notes
scheinen	to shine
der Nebel	fog
die Pflanze, -n	plant
der Wind, -e	wind
der Schnee	snow
es schneit	it's snowing
trocken	dry
naß	wet
das Eis	ice

Seite 75 — Page 75

extrem	extremely
gleichzeitig	at the same time
der Temperaturunterschied, -e	change in temperature
die Wüste, -n	desert
der Golf von Biskaya	Bay of Biscay
bekannt	famous
wohl	→
Bekannt ist wohl der Londoner Nebel.	London's fog is certainly famous.
das Grad, -e	degree

jeden Tag	→ see contrastive notes
gegen Mittag	around noon
das Thermometer, -	thermometer
bis zu	up to
minus	below zero, minus
das Leben	life
das Meer, -e	sea
das Schiff, -e	ship
für kurze Zeit	for a short time
der Regenwald, ⸚er	rain forest
hoch	high, tall
gerade	at the moment, at present
das Gewitter, -	thunderstorm
die Wetterlage, -n	weather condition
das Tief, -s	low
der Osten	East
die Meeresluft	sea air
der Norden	North
das Hoch	high
die Alpen (plural)	the Alps
die Vorhersage, -n	forecast
wolkig	cloudy
ab Nachmittag	from the afternoon (onwards)
Nord-West	Northwest
die Tageshöchsttemperatur, -en	maximum daytime temperature
die Tiefsttemperatur, -en	minimum temperature
um	→
um 10 Grad	around 10 degrees
die Morgenstunde, -n	morning hour
sonst	otherwise
sonnig	sunny
die Tagestemperatur, -en	daytime temperature
Süd-West	Southwest

Seite 76 | Page 76

der Bodensee	Lake Constance
der Ausflug, ⸚e	outing
das Fahrrad, ⸚er	bicycle
baden	to swim
die Gartenparty, -s	garden party
der Spaziergang, ⸚e	walk, stroll

der Wetterbericht, -e	weather report
der Reisewetterbericht, -e	holiday weather report
der Wohnort, -e	place where one lives

Seite 77   Page 77

nachher	afterwards
bei	→
Bei diesem Regen?	In this rain?
da	→ see contrastive notes
Da möchte ich lieber fernsehen.	(In this rain,) I'd rather watch TV.
schon	→
Was der Wetterbericht schon sagt ...!	Who cares what the weather report says ...!
das Fenster, -	window
der Schirm, -e	umbrella
mitnehmen	to take along → see contrastive notes
wie	→
Wie du willst.	As you like.
zurückgehen	to return, to go back
der Strand, ¨e	beach
Wie?	What?
frisch	chilly
draußen	outside
einpacken	to pack

Seite 78   Page 78

das Preisrätsel, -	competition
die Zentrale, -n	center, headquarters
der Fremdenverkehr	tourism
der Handel	trade, commerce
das Land, ¨er	country (nation)
flach	flat
die Nordsee	North Sea
die Ostsee	Baltic Sea
das Mittelgebirge, -	low mountain range
der Wald, ¨er	forest
der Westen	West
der Süden	South
hohe ← hoch	high
überraschen	to surprise

die Bodenfläche	surface area
überall	everywhere
das Quiz	quiz
die Gegend, -en	region
das Nachbarland, ⁻er	neighbouring country
die Landwirtschaft	agriculture
das Gebirge, -	mountain range

Seite 79 / Page 79

das Postfach, ⁻er	post office box
der Einsendeschluß	closing date for entries
die Landschaft, die ...	→ see contrastive notes
der Fluß, Flüsse	river
die Insel, -n	island
der Preis, -e	prize
die Wochenendreise, -n	weekend trip
das Volkslied, -er	folk song
die Landkarte, -n	map
die Grenze, -n	border

Seite 80 / Page 80

der Gipfel, -	hill top, mountain top
die Ruh = die Ruhe	rest, quiet
der Wipfel, -	treetop
spüren	to feel
der Hauch	breeze
das Vögelein, -	little bird
schweigen	to become silent
ruhen	to rest
Rotkäppchen	Little Red Riding Hood
der Wolf, ⁻e	wolf
böse	evil, nasty
der Tannenbaum, ⁻e	fir tree, Christmas tree
das Blatt, ⁻er	leaf
grünen	to be green; to turn green
die Sommerzeit, -en	summertime
das Weihnachtslied, -er	Christmas carol
herauskommen	to come out
hungrig	hungry
sich legen	to lie down

einschlafen	to fall asleep
fällen	to fell, cut down
wachsen	to grow
bewundern	to admire
bedenken	to think (something) over
das Jahrhundert, -e	century
drum (darum)	for that reason
irgendwo	anywhere
der Waldbesucher, -	forest visitor
die Ruhe	rest
die Erholung	recreation
wegwerfen	here: to throw away, to litter
das Forstamt, ¨er	forestry department

Seite 81 | Page 81

schrecklich	terrible
die Zukunftsvision, -en	vision of the future
die Tanne, -n	fir (tree)
die Umweltkatastrophe, -n	environmental catastrophe
die Ursache, -n	cause
der/die Wissenschaftler/in	scientist
das Umweltgift, -e	poison for the environment
der Zitronensaft	lemon juice
dafür	for this
die Luft	air
Die Ursache dafür liegt in der Luft.	The cause for this lies in the air. / The culprit is the air.
zuviel	too much
das Schwefeldioxyd	sulphur dioxide
enthalten	to contain
zu 56% = 56 Prozent	56 per cent
das Kohlekraftwerk, -e	coal fired power station
das Ölkraftwerk, -e	oil fired power station
der Schornstein, -e	chimney
das Abgas, -e	waste gas
weiterbringen	to carry
das Gebiet, -e	area
tausende	thousands
die Ländergrenze, -n	border of a country, international border
exportieren	to export
das Gift, -e	poison

importieren	to import
europäisch	European
das Industriezentrum, -zentren	industrial center
zuviel	too much
die Schwefelsäure	sulphuric acid
flüssig	liquid
aggressiv	aggressive
dadurch	for this reason
konzentrieren	to concentrate
der Giftstoff, -e	toxic substance
aufnehmen	to absorb
doppelt	twice as much
die Fichte, -n	spruce
innerhalb	within

Seite 82	Page 82
entfernt	distant, far away
entstehen	to come into existence
heraussuchen	to pick out
kommentieren	to comment on
die Grafik, -en	graphic, picture
das Resultat, -e	result
der Umweltschutz	protection of the environment
das Plakat, -e	poster
werfen	to throw, to toss
der Hausmüll	household rubbish, trash
gießen	to pour
das Öl	oil
das Altöl	used oil
die Glasflasche, -n	glass bottle
der Glascontainer, -n	glass container
sparen	to save, conserve
die Energie, -n	energy
heizen	to heat
zurücknehmen	to take back
gebrauchen	to use
das Glas	glass
das Altglas	old glass, e. g. non-refundable glass bottles
die Kohle	coal
das Trinkwasser	drinking water

giftig	poisonous, toxic
der Stoff, -e	substance

|---|---|
die Plastikflasche, -n	plastic bottle
die Plastiktüte, -n	plastic bag
das PVC	PVC
verbrennen	to burn
selber	self
uns selber	ourselves, us
das Umweltproblem, -e	environment problem

Contrastive notes

es (page 74): Note that there are two uses of *es*. It can refer to a *das*-noun (e. g. *das Klima*) or it can be the equivalent of the impersonal English *it*.

Der Golf von Biskaya (page 75): Care needs to be taken when translating proper names. Look up *Golf* in a dictionary and you will find *Gulf*. But in an atlas, you will see that this particular piece of water is known as the *Bay of Biscay*.

jeden Tag (pages 75 and 141): As you will observe, German uses the accusative case for expressions of time such as *jeden Tag*. There are more examples on page 141.

da (page 77): Used as a conjunction, *da* can have the sense of *in that case* or *under these circumstances*.

mitnehmen (page 77): In German, you do not need to repeat the pronoun when using *mitnehmen*. *We can take it with us* is simply *Wir können es mitnehmen*.

die Landschaft, die ... (pages 79 and 142): The familiar *der, die* and *das* can be used on their own to introduce a clause; they mean *that* or *who*, and the clause they introduce is a *Relativsatz*. You will find examples on page 142. Note that in these clauses, the main verb again takes the end position. Be careful to select the right gender for the noun to which you are referring. It's *der Mann, der ...*, *die Frau, die ...* and so on. Also note that for Dativ Plural and Genitiv, the *Relativpronomen* differ from the respective articles.

Lektion 7

der Reporter, -	reporter
dabeihaben	to have with one, to have in one's possession
die Guitarre, -n	guitar
der Teddybär, -en	teddy bear
die Kohletablette, -n	charcoal tablet
die Check-Liste, -n	checklist
die Gepäckversicherung, -en	luggage insurance
abschließen	to take out (an insurance policy)
der Krankenschein, -e	medical treatment form
besorgen	to get
der Paß, Pässe	passport
der Ausweis, -e	identification card → see contrastive notes
verlängern	to renew
lassen	→ see contrastive notes
das Visum, Visa	visa
die Katze, -n	cat
untersuchen	to examine
impfen	to vaccinate
der Reiseprospekt, -e	travel brochure
der Fahrplan, ⁻e	schedule, timetable
die Fahrkarte, -n	(bus, train) ticket
die Flugkarte, -n	plane ticket
der Platz, ⁻e	seat
reservieren	to reserve
das Hotelzimmer	hotel room
die Versicherungskarte, -n	insurance card
die Vorbereitung, -en	preparation
wechseln	to exchange
der Reisescheck, -s	traveler's check
die Reinigung, -en	cleaner's
die Wäsche	here: washing (everything that can be washed in the washing machine)
die Apotheke, -n	pharmacy, chemist's → see contrastive notes
das Pflaster, -	sticking plaster

56

die Drogerie, -n	drugstore
die Seife, -n	soap
die Zahnbürste, -n	toothbrush
die Zahnpasta	toothpaste
der Koffer, -	suitcase
packen	to pack
die Wäsche	here: underwear
das Handtuch, ̈er	towel
das Bettuch, ̈er	sheet
das Fluggepäck	flight luggage
der Schlüssel, -	key
zumachen	to close
das Licht	light, electricity
die Heizung	heating

Seite 87   Page 87

die Reiseplanung, -en	planning of a trip
vor	→
vor der Reise	before the journey
das Ferienhaus, ̈er	vacation house
die Geschäftsreise, -n	business trip
der Campingurlaub	camping vacation
das Camping	camping
der Ski, -er	ski
der Ski-Schuh, -e	ski boots
weiterüben	to practise further

Seite 88   Page 88

kurz	→
kurz vor der Grenze	near the border, a short distance from the border
merken	to notice
weder ... noch ...	neither ... nor ...
zurückfahren	to drive back

Seite 89   Page 89

die Gruppe, -n	group
planen	to plan
die Sahara	Sahara (Desert)

der Pazifik	Pacific Ocean
die Antarktis	Antarctica
die Reisegruppe, -n	travel group
das Ding, -e	thing
das Ende	end
am Ende	in the end
der Reiseteilnehmer, -	travel group member
retten	to rescue
die Aluminiumfolie, -n	aluminium foil
der Bleistift, -e	pencil
die Briefmarke, -n	stamp
der Camping-Gasofen	gas stove for camping
das Familienfoto, -s	family picture
der Schnaps	schnaps → see contrastive notes
der Fotoapparat, -e	camera
der Kochtopf, ⁀e	saucepan
der Kompaß, Kompasse	compass
das Blatt, ⁀er	sheet
100 Blatt	100 sheets
die Plastiktasche, -n	plastic bag
das Salz	salt
der Pfeffer	pepper
das Seil, -e	rope
der Spiegel	mirror
das Streichholz, ⁀er	match
die Taschenlampe, -n	torch, flashlight
das Telefonbuch, ⁀er	phone book
die Wolldecke, -n	woollen blanket
vorschlagen	to propose, to suggest
notwendig	necessary
zum Kochen	→ see contrastive notes

Seite 90 / Page 90

das Ausländerkind, -er	foreign child
unter	under, below
der Türke, -n	Turk
vorstellen	to present
die Hauptschulklasse, -n	general school class
türkisch	Turkish
bevor	before
wegfahren	to leave

ausländisch	foreign
übrige	others
wissen, was ...	→ see contrastive notes
fragt, ob ...	→ see contrastive notes

Seite 91 — Page 91

die Klassenreise, -n	class trip
der Schafskäse	sheep's milk cheese
die Olive, -n	olive
die Gastfamilie, -n	host family
das Arbeiterviertel, -	working class quarter (of a city)
fleißig	hard-working
privat	private
die Freundschaft, -en	friendship
der Mitschüler, -	classmate
hoffentlich	hopefully → see contrastive notes
übersetzen	to translate
das Sprachproblem, -e	language problem
die Gasteltern (plural)	host parents
die Geschwister (plural)	brothers and sisters, siblings
die Gastfreundschaft	hospitality
irgendwie	somehow; rather
arm	poor
schon	→
Irgendwie arm sind die schon.	They are rather poor, somehow.
damit	by that
stehen	to stand
erst mal	first of all
der Kunsthändler, -	art dealer
einladen	to invite
Tausend und eine Nacht	The Arabian Nights (Set of Arabian fairy tales)
farbig	coloured
das Glasfenster, -	glass window
farbige Glasfenster	stained-glass-windows
die Lampe, -n	lamp
das Gold	gold
die Wand, ⸚e	wall

der Harem, -s	harem
hinaufgehen	to go up, to go upstairs
der Hausherr	master of the house
streng	strict, strictly
der Koran	Koran
nach	→
nach dem Koran	according to the Koran
erlauben	to permit
reagieren	to react
enttäuscht	disappointed
das Dorfkind, -er	village child
wiedererkennen	to recognize
die Begrüßung, -en	greeting
der Festtag, -e	holiday, festival
die Feier, -n	celebration
der Dorfälteste, -n	village elder
trennen	to separate
das Männerhaus, ¨er	men's house
die Atmosphäre	atmosphere
herzlich	warm, cordial
der Tabak	tobacco
die Art, -en	manner
zuschauen	to look on
sitzen	to sit
einzig	single
interessant	interesting
der Heilige Geist	Holy Ghost
der Gott, ¨er	god
selbst	here: even
der Christ, -en	Christian
der Muslim	Muslim
die Schwerarbeit	hard work
das Glück	luck
zu seinem Glück	luckily for him
dabeisein	to be present
das Hammelfleisch	mutton
der Joghurt	yoghurt
die Pizza	pizza
schrecklich	awful, terrible

so	→
und so	and so forth
die Portion, -en	portion, helping

Seite 93   Page 93

oder	→
Stimmt doch, oder?	That's right, isn't it?
der Faschist, -en	fascist

Seite 94   Page 94

auswandern	to emigrate
um ... zu ...	→ see contrastive notes
damit	→ see contrastive notes
die Steuer, -n	tax
das Land	land, property
bauen	to build
einwandern	to immigrate
das Praktikum, Praktika	practicum, training period
aussteigen	to opt out
einsteigen	to opt in
Nicht "aussteigen", einsteigen in Süd-amerika.	Don't opt out, opt in in South America.
eng	cramped
anderthalb	one and a half
der Platz	space, room
der Landwirtschaftsbetrieb, -e	(large) farm
die Farm, -en	farm
erhalten	to obtain
die Aufenthaltserlaubnis, -se	residence permit
deutschfreundlich	friendly towards Germans and Germany
der Ausländer, -	foreigner
Mio = Million	million
sonstige	others
die Hälfte, -n	half

Seite 95   Page 95

der Auswanderer, -	emigrant
die Welle, -n	wave
die Auswanderer-Welle	wave of emigrants

hunderttausende	hundreds of thousands
verlassen	to leave, to quit
die Auskunft, ⁻e	information
der Preis, -e	here: cost
um	→
um jeden Preis	at any cost
die Botschaft, -en	embassy
das Konsulat, -e	consulate
der Krieg, -e	war
Europa	Europe
hoffen	to hope
die Heimat	homeland
die Freiheit	liberty
der Elektroingenieur, -e	electrical engineer
sich informieren	to gather information
das Wunschland	country of one's choosing
die Arbeitslosigkeit	unemployment
das Glück	happiness, good fortune
der Bäckermeister, -	master baker
zurückfliegen	to fly back

Seite 96	Page 96
die Auswanderung	emigration
über	→
Auskünfte über	information about
das Einwanderungsgesetz, -e	immigration law
die Arbeitserlaubnis	work permit
der Hauskauf, ⁻e	house purchase
der Ratgeber, -	information booklet

Contrastive notes

der Ausweis (page 86): All Germans have an official identity card (with a photograph). This may seem bureaucratic, but it has its practical advantages, for example when the ID card is used to support a cheque or credit card.

lassen (page 86): This can simply mean *to let*, as in *Laß mich das Visum beantragen*. Or it can mean *to let someone do something vor you – Ich lasse meinen Sohn das Auto waschen*. Or – and this is the tricky one for English speakers – you need not say who is going to do the job:

Ich lasse das Auto waschen. Here we would say in English *I am going to have the car washed*, using a past form. Note that in German the second verb stays in the infinitive – the only difference in our last two examples is the absence of *meinen Sohn.*

die Apotheke, die Drogerie (page 86): In Germany, you will find that dispensing chemists *(Apotheke)* are quite separate from the shop where you go for soap, perfumes, shampoo etc. *(Drogerie).* The *Apotheke* specialises in prescribed medicines and will pay more attention to an image of clinical efficiency than to attractive store design.

Schnaps (page 89): This is a general word covering any sort of strong liquor or spirits.

zum Kochen (page 89): German uses *zum* with a verb turned into a noun (i. e. the infinitive with a capital letter) to indicate the purpose for which something is used, e. g. *zum Trinken = for drinking.*

wissen, was ...; fragt, ob ... (pages 90 and 144): When a question becomes part of a longer sentence, its word order changes, with the verb taking the second verb position (at the end of the sentence). You can find several examples of such *Indirekte Fragesätze* on page 144. Note the new *Subjunktor ob* (meaning *if* or *whether*) used when there is no other question word to introduce the question.

hoffentlich (page 91): This is the equivalent (and probably the origin) of the American *hopefully.* British English has to use a phrase such as *Let's hope.*

um ... zu + Infinitiv; damit (pages 94 and 145): German uses *um ... zu ...* whenever English *in order to* is appropriate. Be careful not to confuse it with the *Infinitivsatz mit "zu"* (cf. page 138), which is an *Ergänzung* to a verb like *versuchen, vergessen* etc., whereas an *Infinitivsatz mit "um ... zu"* is always a *Freie Angabe.*
damit, on the other hand, is a *Subjunktor* introducing a *Nebensatz* (in which, as you know, the personal form of the verb takes the second verb position). Its English equivalent would be a clause introduced by *so that.* Of course this is quite different from the use of *damit* as pronominal form meaning *with this, with it.*

Lektion 8

Einw. = der Einwohner, -	inhabitant
die Partei, -en	political party
der Bundestag	Lower House of the Federal Parliament
die Verteilung	distribution
der Sitz, -e	seat

die Presse	(printing) press
die Schlagzeile, -n	headline
das Wahlrecht	voting right
der Gastarbeiter, -	foreign worker
der Fußballstar, -s	soccer star
die Verletzung, -en	injury
der Preiskrieg, -e	price war
die Zigarettenindustrie	cigarette industry
das Stadion, Stadien	stadium
der Fußballverein, -e	soccer club
der Zollbeamte, -n	customs official
der Verkehrsunfall, ̈-e	traffic accident
die Straßenbahn, -en	tram, streetcar
außer	except for
der Fahrer, -	driver
verletzt	injured
das Parlament, -e	parliament
wegen	due to, because of
die Knieoperation, -en	knee operation
gegen	against
der HSV = der Hamburger Sport-Verein	Hamburg Sports Club
der Raucher, -	smoker
die Nachricht, -en	news
die Rubrik, -en	section
der Lokalteil, -e	local section
die Innenpolitik	domestic affairs

64

Seite 100 — Page 100

der Aufzug, ⸚e	elevator, lift
der Briefumschlag, ⸚e	envelope
das Paket, -e	package
das Päckchen, -	small package
liegen bleiben	to be left undelivered
der Poststreik, -s	postal strike
der Lebensmittel-Laden, ⸚	grocery store
die Bäckerei, -en	bakery
der Stadtteil, -e	part of the city
das Ausländergesetz, -e	legislation on foreigners
bleiben	→ see contrastive notes
zerstören	to destroy
das Verkehrsproblem, -e	traffic problem
das Stadtzentrum, -zentren	city centre, downtown

Seite 101 — Page 101

interviewen	to interview
das Ereignis, -se	event
die Wahl, -en	election
die Gefahr, -en	danger
das Land, ⸚er	→ see contrastive notes

Seite 102 — Page 102

der/die Grüne, -n	member of the Green Party
während	while
die/der Abgeordnete, -n	member of the Bundestag or a Landtag
der Bundestag	Lower House of the Federal Parliament
das Abgeordnetengehalt, ⸚er	salary for members of the Bundestag or Landtag
das Demonstrationsgesetz, -e	demonstration legislation
scharf	strict
die Bundesregierung	Federal Government
die Landtagswahl, -en	land, state parliament election
der Landtag	land, state parliament
wählen	to elect
der Ministerpräsident	land, state prime minister
Großbritannien	Great Britain
der Kronprinz	crown prince

britisch	British
die Rheinarmee	(British) Army of the Rhine
der Wirtschaftsminister, -	minister of economic affairs
der Bundesrat	Upper House of the Federal Parliament
das Mehrwertsteuergesetz	legislation on value-added tax
der Bundespräsident	President of the Federal Republic
die Bundeshauptstadt	Federal Capital
der Sprecher	spokesman
das System, -e	system

Seite 103 — Page 103

das Wahlsystem, -e	electoral system
repräsentativ	representative
die Landesregierung, -en	land, state government
die Parlamentskammer, -n	chamber of Parliament
der Wähler, -	voter
der Bundesbürger, -	citizen of the Federal Republic
ab	→
ab 18 Jahre	18 years and older
der Regierungschef, -s	head of government
das Regionalparlament, -e	regional parliament
der Staatschef, -s	head of state

Seite 104 — Page 104

die Republik, -en	republic
das Reich	empire
parlamentarisch	parliamentary
die Demokratie, -n	democracy
sozialistisch	socialist
die Monarchie, -n	monarchy
das Wirtschaftssystem, -e	economic system
neutral	neutral
der Staat, -en	state, country
der Bündnispartner, -	ally
die UdSSR	USSR
der Außenminister, -	foreign affairs minister

Seite 105 — Page 105

die Wiedervereinigung	reunification

statt	instead of
die Wiederbewaffnung	rearmament
ungeteilt	undivided
das Vaterland, ̈er	fatherland
die Nachkriegsgeschichte	post-war history
seit	→ see contrastive notes
der Weltkrieg, -e	world war
die Regierung, -en	government
die Sowjetunion	Soviet Union
der Friedensvertrag, ̈e	peace treaty
der Alliierte, -n	ally
der Plan, ̈e	plan
abhängig	dependent
der Ostermarsch	Easter march

Seite 106 — Page 106

der Unterschied, -e	difference
die Armee, -n	army
das Mitglied, -er	member
der Pakt	pact
die Nato	NATO
protestieren	to protest
die Atomwaffe, -n	nuclear weapon
der Wirtschaftskontakt, -e	economic contact
der Grundlagenvertrag, ̈e	basic agreement, fundamental treaty
bestätigen	to acknowledge
die/der Bundesdeutsche	citizen of the Federal Republic
der Nachbarstaat, -en	neighboring country
offen	here: unresolved
die Nation, -en	nation
DGB = der Deutsche Gewerkschaftsbund	Federation of German Trade Unions
verhandeln	to negotiate
erstellen	to draw up
die Zeitleiste, -n	chronology

Seite 107 — Page 107

von ... bis ...	from ... until ...
die Beziehung, -en	relationship
Tausende	thousands (of people)
der Konflikt, -e	conflict

die Geschichte	history
temporal	temporal, of time
die Jahreszahl, -en	the year (e. g. 1985)
der Wochentag, -e	day of the week

Contrastive notes

bleiben (page 100): Note that the English verb *to stay* must be rendered in German by two different verbs: *wohnen* and *bleiben*. The verb *bleiben* must be used when the staying is seen as *not moving out, not moving on, not leaving; wohnen* is used when it is a matter of *having accommodation* (flat, room, house, hotel etc.).

das Land (page 101): Here *Land* is used in the general sense of *country*. But on the following page, you will find it used in a more specific sense, to mean one of the member states *(Länder)* that make up the Federal Republic of Germany.

seit (page 105): Note that in German after a phrase begun by *seit*, the sentence continues in the tense which would have been used even if the *seit*-phrase were not there, while in English we have to use a rather clumsier construction:
Seit vierzig Jahren wohne ich in Berlin.
For the last forty years, I have been living in Berlin.

Lektion 9

Seite 110	Page 110
das Dach, ¨-er	roof
seit	→
Wir wohnen seit vier Jahren zusammen.	We have been living together for four years.
sich ausziehen	to get undressed
die Oma, -s	grandma
der Opa, -s	grandpa
unglücklich	unhappy
danken	to thank

die Schulaufgaben (plural)	homework
zum Glück	fortunately
mir	→ see contrastive notes
der Altenclub, -s	senior citizens' club
mitschicken	to enclose

Seite 111 — Page 111

das Reflexivpronomen, -	reflexive pronoun
weiterarbeiten	to continue working
der Lebensabend	later years of life
das Seniorenheim, -e	senior citizens' home
das Kleinappartement, -s	small appartement
zum Teil	here: some
der Pensionär, -e	pensioner
sich einrichten	to get installed, to settle (in a room, flat etc.)
die Hilfe	help
das Sekretariat, -e	administrative office

Seite 112 — Page 112

das Seniorentreffen, -	senior citizens' get-together
das Alter	age
die Rente, -n	pension
verwitwet	widowed
die Krise, -n	crisis
durchschnittlich	on average
die Alterslast	burden caused by the aged
wachsen	to grow
steigend	rising
der Beitrag, ⁻e	contribution
sinkend	sinking, diminishing
das Rentenniveau	pension level
rechnen	to calculate
gehen	→
Das geht.	That's possible.

Seite 113 — Page 113

| der Möbelschreiner, - | carpenter |
| regieren | to rule |

ernst	serious
neben	aside from, besides
der Haushalt, -e	running the home
das Klavier, -e	piano
spielen	to play
zu Fuß	on foot
sich beeilen	to hurry
backen	to bake
ausschneiden	to cut out
der Zettel, -	slip of paper
ständig	constantly
der Elektroofen, ⁻	electric oven
der Ofen, ⁻	oven
die Steckdose, -n	(electric) socket
der Hof, ⁻e	yard
das Holzregal, -e	wooden shelf
das Gästezimmer, -	guest room
der Assistent, -en	assistant

Seite 114 — Page 114

mir das – es dir	→ see contrastive notes
der Moment, -e	moment
Moment!	Just a moment!
die Farbe, -n	paint
das Holz, ⁻er	wood
die Bürste, -n	brush
der/die Bekannte, -n	acquaintance, friend → see contrastive notes
die Karte, -n	card
Karten spielen	to play cards
der Verein, -e	club, society

Seite 115 — Page 115

die Büroarbeit, -en	office work
der Versicherungskaufmann, -kaufleute	insurance salesman
das Abenteuer, -	adventure
verkaufen	to sell
gebraucht	used
das Kanu, -s	canoe
frisch	newly

70

die Laborantin, -nen	Laboratory assistant
starten	to start
fliegend	flying
die Fotosafari, -s	photo safari
im Moment	at the moment

eisern	iron
"die Eisernen"	those who can celebrate their 65th ("iron") wedding anniversary
feiern	to celebrate
silbern	silver
die Silberne Hochzeit	silver wedding anniversary (25th)
golden	golden
die Goldene Hochzeit	golden wedding anniversary (50th)
der/die Glückliche, -n	fortunate person
gemeinsam	shared
erleben	to experience
die Eiserne Hochzeit	iron wedding anniversary (65th)
die Postkarte, -n	postcard
der Liebesbrief, -e	love letter
so	→
Das war so: ...	It was like this: ...
vorbeikommen	to come by
sich setzen	to sit down
... ob sie sich zu uns setzen dürfen.	... whether they could sit down with us.
akzeptieren	to accept
der Heiratsurlaub	wedding leave (from the army)
ungewöhnlich	unusual
die Traumehe	dream marriage
gern haben	to like, to be fond of
vorbei	past, over
stundenlang	for hours
der Tanzsalon, -s	dance salon
der Schlosser, -	locksmith
der Wochenlohn, ⸚e	weekly pay
der Rückblick	→
im Rückblick	in retrospect
stolz	proud
der Eherekord, -e	marriage record

nachmachen	to copy
Das soll mir erst einer nachmachen!	Let's see someone else do that!
das Erinnerungsfoto, -s	souvenir photo
stammen von	here: to date from
der Blick, -e	glance
Liebe auf den ersten Blick	love at first glance
der Jurist, -en	lawyer
die Liebeserklärung, -en	declaration of love
noch mal	again
die Trennung, -en	separation
verreist	gone away on a trip

Seite 118	Page 118
der Ehepartner, -	marriage partner
das Stichwort, -e	key word
kürzen	to shorten
das Familienfest, -e	family celebration
die Liebesgeschichte, -n	love story
einsam	lonely
die Nichtraucherin, -nen	non-smoker (f.)
der Tänzer, -	dancer
sich verabreden	to make a date
sich verloben	to become engaged
sich besuchen	→ see contrastive notes
sich streiten	to quarrel
sich verlieben	to fall in love

Contrastive notes

mir (page 110): We met earlier (Lektion 3) a group of verbs which require a reflexive pronoun (*mich, sich* etc.) to complete their meaning. In this *Lektion* we encounter a second group, where the action is not done to oneself but for oneself; here German uses a Dative. These include phrases like *Ich koche mir mein Essen,* which translates as *I cook myself a meal,* but it is clearly *the meal,* not *myself,* which is the object. Note that in the Dative, too, the reflexive pronoun for the third person and the polite *Sie* is *sich.*

es – das (pages 114 and 150): You can see from the charts on page 150 how word order can be used to emphasise certain word(s) in a sentence. Where two object pronouns are both unemphasised, the accusative always precedes the dative. If a pronoun and a noun phrase are both used as objects, the pronoun will precede the noun phrase regardless of which is in which case.

der Bekannte (page 114): Particularly among younger people, the words *Freund* and *Freundin* when applied to a member of the opposite sex can imply something much closer than the English word *friend*. So Germans tend to use *der/die Bekannte* where a more casual friendship is implied.

sich besuchen (pages 118 and 149): Sometimes a reflexive pronoun is used where the action is not reflexive but reciprocal. *Sie besuchen sich.* does not mean *They go and see themselves.*, but of course *They go and see each other.* You will find more examples on page 149.

Lektion 10

Seite 121	Page 121
der Reim, -e	rhyme
der Baukasten, ⁼	construction kit
das Boot, -e	boat
ziehen	to move
weich	soft
der Sand	sand
bunt	colorful
breit	wide
der Vogel, ⁼	bird
rufen	to call
zählen	to count
das Gedicht, -e	poem
der Titel, -	title
der Mai	May

Seite 122	Page 122
der Herbsttag, -e	day in fall/autumn
wachen	to lie awake
die Allee, -n	avenue
hin und her	back and forth
das Blatt, ⁼er	leaf

treiben	to drift
wunderschön	most beautiful
die Knospe, -n	bud
springen	to burst
das Herz, -en	heart
aufgehen	here: to burst (open)
gestehen	to confess
sehnen	to yearn
das Sehnen	yearning
verlangen	to crave, to desire
das Verlangen	longing
die Vergänglichkeit, -en	transitoriness
taumelbunt	giddily colourful
müd = müde	here: weary
trunken	drunk (only lyrically)
das Harfenmädchen	girl with a harp
vergehen	to pass, to fade
mein	mine
der Rauch	smoke
fehlen	→
Fehlte er, ...	If it was absent ...
trostlos	bleak

Seite 123 — Page 123

die Boutique, -n	boutique
wunderbar	wonderful
das Urlaubsland, ⸚er	vacation land
die Burg, -en	castle
das Kloster, ⸚	monastery, convent
dorthin	(to) there
gehen	→
zu Fuß gehen	to walk
die Treppe, -n	stairs
das Kochbuch, ⸚er	cookbook
der Feiertag, -e	holiday
das Kunstmuseum, -museen	art museum
das Gemälde, -	painting
die Handzeichnung, -en	drawing
der Frühstückstisch, -e	breakfast table
sie habe ← haben (Konjunktiv I)	she has (indirectly quoting someone else's words)

74

der Mord, -e	murder
begehen	to commit
der Kriminalroman, -e	detective novel
die Hand, ⁻e	hand
zur Hand nehmen	to pick up
das Hobby-Buch, ⁻er	hobby book
das Reisebuch, ⁻er	travel book
das Kunstbuch, ⁻er	art book
das Sportbuch, ⁻er	sports book

Seite 124   Page 124

der Comic, -s	comic strip book
frisch	→
die frische Luft	fresh air
der Inhalt, -e	contents
sich erinnern	to remember

Seite 125   Page 125

das Reich	realm
die Phantasie	fantasy
das Amphitheater, -	amphitheatre
eines Tages	one day → see contrastive notes
die Lebenszeit	time out of people's life
der Meister, -	master
geheimnisvoll	mysterious
der Verwalter, -	custodian
das Menschenkind, -er	man-child, human child
stillstehen	to stand still
kämpfen	to fight
der Bestseller, -	bestseller
die Rose, -n	rose
unendlich	neverending
trotz alledem	in spite of all this
der Ring, -e	ring

Seite 126   Page 126

näher	→
aus der näheren Umgebung	from the immediate neighborhood
die Umgebung, -en	neighborhood

ausfragen	to interrogate
gegenüberstehen	to stand across from
ängstlich	anxiously
erwarten	to expect
versichern	to assure
unbestimmt	uncertain
die Bewegung, -en	movement
irgendwohin	somewhere or other → see contrastive notes
forschen	to inquire
anschauen	to look at
ratlos	helpless
hob ← heben	to lift
die Schultern heben	to shrug
seufzen	to sigh
fortfahren	to continue
nennen	to name
soweit	as far as

Seite 127	Page 127
halten für	to take for
... weil sie es für einen Spaß hielten.	... because they took it as a joke.
	→ see contrastive notes
ernsthaft	seriously
unsicher	uncertain
gedankenverloren	lost in thought
jedenfalls	in any case
anfassen	to touch
festhalten	to hold fast
immerzu	all the time
herkommen	to come from
hinführen	to lead to
jene/jener/jenes	that
der Textteil, -e	part of a text
die Zusammenfassung, -en	summary
wozu	→
Wozu passen sie?	Where do they fit?

die Schulklasse, -n	school class
kommen auf	to get the idea of
Tag und Nacht	day and night
bestehen in	to consist of
eigentlich	actual
die Geduld	patience
niederschreiben	to write down
rasch	quickly
sich entscheiden	to decide
die Hetze	haste
lebendig	alive
sich ausdenken	to think up
handeln von	to deal with
gerade	exactly, just → see contrastive notes
sich wundern	to be astonished, to find strange
immerfort	constantly
die Schildkröte, -n	tortoise

Contrastive notes

eines Tages (page 125): Some phrases of time contain constructions in the Genitive case; these are slightly archaic, but you will still find them particularly in literary German. A less common one is *eines Mittags* (page 126).

irgendwohin (page 126): The compounds with *irgend-* always imply a vagueness, so *irgendwohin* is *somewhere or other, irgendetwas something or other*, etc.

halten für (page 127): This is a particularly good example of a phrasal verb, and of the problems it can cause. If you try to look it up in a dictionary, you may have difficulty finding it. But the meaning *to take as* or *to take for* is so different from the other meanings of *halten* that a good dictionary will list it somewhere!

gerade (page 128): This adverb has various meanings. Here it means *exactly – That's exactly what my next book is about*. But it can also indicate what the speaker is just doing or has just done, e.g. *Ich habe gerade ein Buch von Michael Ende gelesen.*

Index of items included in Contrastive Notes

The following list includes all items dealt with in Contrastive Notes for Themen 1 and Themen 2. After the item, the first number given indicates which book, and the second number which Lektion, contains the appropriate note

aber 1.2
accusative 1.4
adjective endings 2.1
als 2.5
am besten 1.6
an, auf, in 1.6
die Apotheke 2.7
auf Wiedersehen, auf Wiederhören 1.1
der Ausweis 2.7

der Bahnsteig 2.1
der Bekannte 2.9
bekommen 2.5
der Besuch 2.5
der Betriebsrat 2.4
bitte schön 1.4
bleiben, wohnen 2.8

comparison 2.4
compound verbs 1.4

da 1.5; 2.6
damit, um ... zu 2.7
das ist 1.3
daß 2.5
Dativ 1.7
dauernd 2.5
denn 1.2
der, die, das 1.3
der (pronoun) 1.7
die Möbel 1.3
doch 1.2; 1.3; 1.7
du 1.3
dürfen, sollen, wollen 1.9

ein, kein 1.3
eines Tages 2.10
eins, einen 1.7
er, sie, es 1.3
erst 1.2
es 2.6
es gibt 1.2
expressions of time 2.6

fahren 1.6
feminine forms in -in 1.2
die Flasche 1.4
Frau 1.1
früh 2.4

ganz 2.2
gefallen 1.3
gemütlich 2.1
Genitiv 2.5
gerade 2.10
gern 1.4
gern mögen, möchte 2.5
grüß dich 1.9
guten Tag 1.1

hallo 1.2
halten ... für 2.10
hatte, war 1.10
hoffentlich 2.7

ich 1.1
IG 2.4
ihr 1.3
immer größer 1.8

imperative 1.4
in + accusative 1.5
indirect questions 2.5
inversion 1.4
irgend- 2.10

ja 2.1
jeder, dieser 2.1
jemand 1.5

kann, muß 1.5
Kirchensteuer 2.4
kündigen 2.1

das Land 2.8
lassen 2.7
liegt 1.3

mal 2.1; 2.2
man 1.1
mitnehmen 2.6
möchte 1.2
mögen 1.7
montag abend 1.5
morgens, mittags 1.9
müssen 1.9

nämlich 1.10
names, translation of 2.5
nehmen 1.4
noch 1.4; 1.5
nouns, capital letters 1.1
nun mal 2.3

perfect tense 1.9
plurals 1.4
Präteritum 2.5
present tense 1.2
professions, no article 1.2

reflexives – reciprocals 2.9
relative pronoun 2.6

Schnaps 2.7
schon 1.2; 2.5
schools and colleges 2.2
schwimmen gehen 1.5
sehr geehrt 2.2
sein, ihr 1.9
seit 1.2; 2.8
separable verbs 1.5
sich 2.3
sie 1.1
situation, movement 1.8
solch 2.3
sondern 1.3
Stück 2.4
subordinate clauses 2.2
suchen 1.3
sympathisch 2.1

das Tarifgespräch 2.4
times 1.5

von 2.4

wäre, hätte 2.3
wann, wenn 2.2
was für, wofür 2.1
weil 2.2
welcher 1.6
werden 2.4
das Werkzeug 2.4
wissen, kennen 1.7
wohin 1.5
wohl 1.7
word order 1.1; 1.6; 2.2
word order – emphasis 2.9
worüber, darüber 2.3
würde 2.3

zu + Dativ 1.8
zu + infinitive 2.5
zum + verb 2.7

LESETEXTE DEUTSCH

Eine Reihe von einfachen oder vereinfachten Texten für Deutschlernende, herausgegeben und bearbeitet von Edith und Albert Schmitz.

Die Lesetexte bieten unterhaltsame, spannende Lektüre für den Kursunterricht oder für das Selbststudium. Die Reihe gliedert sich sprachlich in drei Niveaustufen.

Anruf für einen Toten
Kriminalgeschichten
88 Seiten, mit Zeichnungen, gh.   ISBN 3–19–001343–8

Rübezahl und das kleine Mädchen
Sagen und Märchen
52 Seiten, mit Zeichnungen gh.   ISBN 3–19–001378–0

Schläft wohl gern länger
Jugendgeschichten
64 Seiten, mit Zeichnungen, gh.   ISBN 3–19–001395–0

Der Tag davor
Science-fiction. Erzählungen über die Zukunft
56 Seiten, mit Zeichnungen, gh.   ISBN 3–19–001345–4

Ein Platz für Elefanten
Tiergeschichten
72 Seiten, mit Zeichnungen, gh.   ISBN 3–19–001347–0

Fliegen, wo kein Vogel mehr fliegt
Abenteuergeschichten
56 Seiten, mit Zeichnungen, gh.   ISBN 3–19–001348–9

Start mit Schwierigkeiten
Reiseerzählungen
60 Seiten, mit Zeichnungen, gh.   ISBN 3–19–001379–9

Einer wie ich
Geschichten aus der Welt des Sports
72 Seiten, mit Fotos und Zeichnungen, gh.   ISBN 3–19–001397–7

Max Hueber Verlag · München